THIRD EDITION

DISCOVER YOUR GIFTS

AND LEARN HOW TO USE THEM

ALVIN J. VANDER GRIEND

STUDENT BOOK

FAITH ALIVE® Christian Resources

Grand Rapids, Michigan

We are grateful to Alvin J. Vander Griend for his contributions in planning and revising this third edition of *Discover Your Gifts and Learn How to Use Them* (revised and expanded from *Discover Your Gifts*, first published by Christian Reformed Home Missions in 1980 and updated in 1983, then revised by Faith Alive in 1996).

We also acknowledge with gratitude the gifts of the following persons who contributed to earlier editions: advisors to the original *Discover Your Gifts* were Cliff Christians, David Holwerda, Norman Meyer, and Marion Snapper. Wesley Smedes and Dirk Hart made significant contributions as members of CRC Home Missions staff. Henry De Rooy was project coordinator. Consultants for the 1983 update were Del Nykamp and Mike McGervey, and Edi Bajema provided editorial assistance. David Armstrong, Carl Bosma, Phil Noordmans, Jackie Timmer, Henry Wildeboer, and Randal Young served as advisors for the 1996 edition. Don McCrory served as editor for that edition, and Duncan McIntosh provided input as a denominational leader and spiritual-gifts trainer. Appreciation is due also to thirty pastors and churches who field-tested the material prior to publication of the 1996 edition.

In presenting this 2008 edition, we thank Neil Carlson of the Center for Social Research at Calvin College for assessing the Discover Your Gifts Survey, and we thank Bob Rozema, former curriculum editor at Faith Alive, for pedagogical counsel on revising lessons and other elements. In addition, we thank numerous church leaders, course participants, and other consultants whose responses to surveys and evaluations helped shape this third edition.

Unless otherwise indicated, the Scripture quotations in this publication are from the Holy Bible, Today's New International Version™ (TNIV). © 2001, 2005, International Bible Society. All rights reserved worldwide.

We welcome your comments. Call us at 1-800-333-8300 or e-mail us at editors@faithaliveresources.org.

ISBN 978-1-59255-409-6

5 4 3 2

Mixed Sources
Product group from well-managed forests and other controlled sources
www.fsc.org Cert no. SW-COC-002283
FSC © 1996 Forest Stewardship Council

CONTENTS

Part C: Gift Studies

Part D: Follow-up Tools

INTRODUCTION

God in his grace has given each believer spiritual gifts. In this course you will learn what spiritual gifts are, why God has given them, how they are to be used, and how they can be misused. You'll also learn about the spiritual gifts *you've* been given, including potential gifts that God is working in you to develop. *Discover Your Gifts and Learn How to Use Them* is intended to help you and other believers use your gifts constructively together to the glory of God.

There are four parts to this book:

Part A: Gift Sessions includes five study sessions on spiritual gifts. Each session includes a Bible discovery section, time for instruction, and an opportunity for personal sharing. A Discover Your Gifts Survey is included in this section (and is also available online) for use after session 2.

Part B: FAQs About Spiritual Gifts covers many frequently asked questions people raise about spiritual gifts.

Part C: Gift Studies contains studies of the spiritual gifts featured in this course. Each study includes a definition of the gift, scriptural background, how the gift may be used responsibly and misused, an exploring Scripture exercise, and more. These studies are designed *to be used by participants on their own.*

Part D: Follow-up Tools includes a Waiting Gifts Survey and a Ready to Serve! form for reporting to your church or administrator.

God intends each believer to be a channel of his grace to others. Using our spiritual gifts is one of the primary ways we fulfill this function in God's kingdom. *Discover Your Gifts and Learn How to Use Them* is a proven tool for learning your "spiritual job description" and becoming an instrument of God's grace in this needy world.

You are beginning an exciting and challenging journey. Pray that God will give you the courage and perseverance to complete it. God wants you to be effective and fruitful in the work of his kingdom, and God is most eager to support and strengthen you as you work with other believers to build up the body of Christ.

GUIDELINES

The following guidelines will help you make the best use of this material.

1. **Take the challenge of the course seriously.** The main challenge is not simply to learn about spiritual gifts. It is to discover your gifts and to put them to use in the kingdom of God. God desires and expects our best. That means giving our best in this course and in using our grace-given gifts for God.

2. **Participate freely in the small group discussions and activities.** Every class session provides an opportunity to work in small groups. This gives everyone an opportunity to give input and ask questions. Jump into small group times with a bit of "reckless abandon." Share yourself and your thoughts as freely and fully as possible. Openly accept others and their contributions. In a learning context all questions and comments are valuable.

3. **Read through the FAQs section (Part B) of this book.** The frequently asked questions in Part B are divided into five sections that correspond with the subject matter of this course's five sessions. Studying from these pages after each session will enhance what you have learned in class.

4. **Learn more about individual gifts in the Gifts Studies section (Part C) of this book.** You'll grow to understand more about God's plan for spiritual gifts, the Christian community, your spiritually gifted friends, and yourself.

5. **When the course is finished, look for opportunities to use your gifts in ministry** if you aren't already doing so. Take a careful look at ministry options for which you are best suited. Learn all that you can about them. Talk to and walk alongside those who are in similar kinds

of ministry. This is one of the best ways to find a ministry in which you can use your gifts. Be willing to start small. It may be best to work in an apprentice role first.

6. **Get support.** No ministry should be without support. Start by seeking out the prayer support of other interested individuals. Look for others in similar ministries with whom you can share your thoughts and ask questions. This will take some extra time, but in the long run your ministry in Christ will benefit greatly from the support of other believers.

GIFT SESSIONS

WHAT THE BIBLE SAYS ABOUT SPIRITUAL GIFTS

Opening Prayer

Preview

In this session we will

- discover what the Bible has to say about spiritual gifts.

- answer several basic questions about gifts from Scripture.

- unpack a biblically based definition of spiritual gifts.

Warm-up Exercise

In small groups of three or four persons, introduce yourselves to each other. Tell the others in your group about one of the best gifts you ever received and what made it special. Or you might wish to share why you're taking this course and what you hope will result from it.

Bible Discovery

Read the following Bible passages on spiritual gifts in your small group. Answer the discovery questions that follow each passage and make a note of your answers.

Do as much as you can in the time you're given, but don't worry if you don't make it all the way through. There will be time to discuss everyone's responses in the next part of the lesson, and you can always finish completing your answers at home.

Romans 12:4-8

   ⁴For just as each of us has one body with many members, and these members do not all have the same function, ⁵so in Christ we, though many, form one body, and each member belongs to all the others. ⁶We have different gifts, according to the grace given to each of us. If your gift is prophesying, then prophesy in accordance with your faith; ⁷if it is serving, then serve; if it is teaching, then teach; ⁸if it is to encourage, then give encouragement; if it is giving, then give generously; if it is to lead, do it diligently; if it is to show mercy, do it cheerfully.

1. What does the body metaphor in verses 5 and 6 teach us about gifts in the church?

2. What does grace have to do with spiritual gifts?

3. If you have one of the gifts mentioned here, what does God want you to do with it? What do you think might happen if you attempt a ministry but don't have a gift for it?

4. Underline the gifts mentioned in this passage. Did you encounter any surprises here? If so, explain.

1 Corinthians 12:4-14, 27-28; 13:1-3

   ⁴There are different kinds of gifts, but the same Spirit distributes them. ⁵There are different kinds of service, but the same Lord. ⁶There are different kinds of working, but in all of them and in everyone it is the same God at work.

   ⁷Now to each one the manifestation of the Spirit is given for the common good. ⁸To one there is given through the Spirit a message of wisdom, to another a message of knowledge by means of the same Spirit, ⁹to another faith by the same Spirit, to another gifts of healing by that one Spirit, ¹⁰to another miraculous powers, to another prophecy, to another distinguishing between spirits, to another speaking in different kinds of tongues, and to still another the interpretation of tongues. ¹¹All these are the work of one and the same Spirit, and he distributes them to each one, just as he determines.

[12]Just as a body, though one, has many parts, but all its many parts form one body, so it is with Christ. [13]For we were all baptized by one Spirit so as to form one body—whether Jews or Gentiles, slave or free—and we were all given the one Spirit to drink. [14]Even so the body is not made up of one part but of many. . . .

[27]Now you are the body of Christ, and each one of you is a part of it. [28]And God has placed in the church first of all apostles, second prophets, third teachers, then miracles, then gifts of healing, of helping, of guidance [administration, leadership], and of different kinds of tongues. . . .

[13:1]If I speak in human or angelic tongues, but do not have love, I am only a resounding gong or a clanging cymbal. [2]If I have the gift of prophecy and can fathom all mysteries and all knowledge, and if I have a faith that can move mountains, but do not have love, I am nothing. [3]If I give all I possess to the poor and give over my body to hardship that I may boast, but do not have love, I gain nothing.

1. Who decides what spiritual gifts each believer receives?

2. Who might be expected to have spiritual gifts?

3. Who benefits from spiritual gifts?

4. How are gifted believers like the parts of a human body? (See also Romans 12:4-5 above.)

5. Underline the different gifts mentioned in these verses. Any surprises? Which ones were also mentioned in Romans 12?

Ephesians 4:11-13

[11]So Christ himself gave the apostles, the prophets, the evangelists, the pastors and teachers, [12]to equip his people for works of service, so that the body of Christ may be built up [13]until we all reach unity in the faith and in the knowledge of the Son of God and become mature, attaining to the whole measure of the fullness of Christ.

1. Notice that in verse 11 people themselves are described as gifts to the church. How do the gifted persons mentioned here serve Christ's people—that is, the body of Christ?

2. In what ways will the body of Christ benefit when equipped believers do "works of service"?

3. Underline the gifts mentioned in this passage. Which ones were already mentioned in previous passages?

1 Peter 4:8-11

8Above all, love each other deeply, because love covers over a multitude of sins. 9Offer hospitality to one another without grumbling. 10Each of you should use whatever gift you have received to serve others, as faithful stewards of God's grace in its various forms. 11If you speak, you should do so as one who speaks the very words of God. If you serve, you should do so with the strength God provides, so that in all things God may be praised through Jesus Christ. To him be the glory and the power for ever and ever. Amen.

1. What should we do with our spiritual gifts?

2. What is our ultimate aim when we use our gifts?

3. Which gifts are mentioned in this passage?

Pulling Our Thoughts Together

Now that we've taken a look at some key Bible passages about gifts, let's answer some basic questions together.

Spiritual Gifts
- What are spiritual gifts?

- Who gives these gifts?

- To whom are they given?

- Why are they given?

- Where do they function?

- How do they function?

Unpacking a Definition

Spiritual gifts are special abilities given by Christ through the Holy Spirit to empower believers for the ministries of the body.

- special abilities—

- given by Christ—

- through the Holy Spirit—

- to empower believers—

- for the ministries of the body—

Looking Ahead

In this section of each session you'll find things to do at home that will make these sessions more meaningful to you.

- Read the broader contexts of the Bible passages studied in this first session (from Rom. 12; 1 Cor. 12-13; Eph. 4; 1 Pet. 4). This will help you better understand the Bible's basic teaching on spiritual gifts and prepare you for the sessions that follow.

- Begin reading FAQs About Spiritual Gifts in Part B of this book (section 1 of the FAQs corresponds with session 1, and so on). The insights you find there will help to affirm and expand on what you have learned in this session.

Closing

Three ways to pray:

- *Praise* God as the almighty gift-giving God. All the abilities in spiritual gifts are extensions of God's power.

- *Thank* Jesus Christ and the Holy Spirit for the special abilities given by means of spiritual gifts to all members of the church.

- *Ask* for the Holy Spirit's wisdom and insight in understanding what spiritual gifts are and why they are given to the church. (See James 1:5.)

DISCOVERING MY SPIRITUAL GIFTS

Opening Prayer

Preview

In this session we will

- define and explain several spiritual gifts.

- recognize some of these gifts in others and in ourselves.

- distinguish gifts from talents, fruit, offices, and roles.

Bible Discovery

Let's look more closely at a variety of spiritual gifts cited in Scripture. Note that while the gifts highlighted in this course are those most commonly found in the Bible, others may be identified, and other names for the gifts may be used.

Prophecy

The Spirit-given ability to receive and communicate a message from God so that believers may be edified and encouraged and unbelievers convinced.

Romans 12:6—*If your gift is prophesying, then prophesy in accordance with your faith.*

- The basic idea of this gift is . . .

- Do you know (or know of) someone who has this gift? If so, who?

Service (Helping)
The Spirit-given ability to see and meet the needs of others by willingly helping them in practical ways.

Romans 12:7 —*If [your gift] is serving, then serve.*
(Also referred to as "helping" in 1 Cor. 12:28.)

- The basic idea of this gift is . . .

- Do you know (or know of) someone who has this gift? If so, who?

Teaching
The Spirit-given ability to clearly and effectively communicate biblical truths and information to help believers grow in faith, building up the body of Christ.

Romans 12:7—*If [your gift] is teaching, then teach.*
(See also Eph. 4:11-12.)

- The basic idea of this gift is . . .

- Do you know (or know of) someone who has this gift? If so, who?

Encouragement
The Spirit-given ability to effectively encourage, comfort, challenge, or rebuke others to help them live lives worthy of God.

Romans 12:8—*If [your gift] is to encourage, then give encouragement.*

- The basic idea of this gift is . . .

- Do you know (or know of) someone who has this gift? If so, who?

Giving

The Spirit-given ability to contribute significant personal and material resources to the Lord's work freely, cheerfully, and sacrificially.

Romans 12:8—*If [your gift] is giving, then give generously.*

- The basic idea of this gift is . . .

- Do you know (or know of) someone who has this gift? If so, who?

Leadership

The Spirit-given ability to lead others by seeing and casting a ministry vision, setting and communicating goals, and inspiring and directing people to work together toward those goals.

Romans 12:8—*If [your gift] is to lead, do it diligently.*

- The basic idea of this gift is . . .

- Do you know (or know of) someone who has this gift? If so, who?

Mercy

The Spirit-given ability to feel empathy and compassion for hurting people and to translate that feeling into cheerful acts of service.

Romans 12:8—*If [your gift] is to show mercy, do it cheerfully.*

- The basic idea of this gift is . . .

- Do you know (or know of) someone who has this gift? If so, who?

Administration

The Spirit-given ability to design and execute a plan of action through which a number of believers are enabled to work effectively together to do the Lord's work.

1 Corinthians 12:28—*God has placed in the church . . . gifts of . . . guidance [administration].*

- The basic idea of this gift is . . .

- Do you know (or know of) someone who has this gift? If so, who?

Evangelism

The Spirit-given ability to present the gospel to unbelievers in clear and meaningful ways that bring a positive response.

Ephesians 4:11—*Christ himself gave . . . evangelists . . . to equip his people. . . .*

- The basic idea of this gift is . . .

- Do you know (or know of) someone who has this gift? If so, who?

Shepherding (Pastoring)

The Spirit-given ability to watch over, care for, and feed members of the body of Christ, guiding, admonishing, and discipling them toward spiritual maturity.

Ephesians 4:11—*Christ himself gave . . . pastors [shepherds] . . . to equip his people. . . .*

- The basic idea of this gift is . . .

- Do you know (or know of) someone who has this gift? If so, who?

Intercession

The Spirit-given ability to pray faithfully and effectively for others for extended periods and to see many specific answers to those prayers.

Ephesians 6:18—*Pray in the Spirit on all occasions with all kinds of prayers and requests. With this in mind, be alert and always keep on praying for all the Lord's people.*

Colossians 4:12—*Epaphras . . . is always wrestling in prayer for you, that you may stand firm in all the will of God, mature and fully assured.*

- The basic idea of this gift is . . .

- Do you know (or know of) someone who has this gift? If so, who?

Hospitality
The Spirit-given ability to welcome and graciously serve guests and strangers so that they feel at home.

1 Peter 4:8-9—*Above all, love each other deeply, because love covers over a multitude of sins. Offer hospitality to one another without grumbling.*

- The basic idea of this gift is . . .

- Do you know (or know of) someone who has this gift? If so, who?

Creative Ability
The Spirit-given ability to communicate truth and advance God's kingdom creatively through music, drama, visual arts, and/or writing skills.

Exodus 35:31-33—*He has filled [them] with the Spirit of God . . . to engage in all kinds of artistic crafts.*

- The basic idea of this gift is . . .

- Do you know (or know of) someone who has this gift? If so, who?

Personal Sharing
In small groups of three or four persons, share your thoughts about the gifts you've covered in this session.

- Did any of these gifts or the definitions of gifts surprise you? If so, in what way?

- Which of these gifts do you think you might have?

What's Distinctive About Spiritual Gifts?

- How do spiritual gifts differ from natural talents?

- How are spiritual gifts different from the fruit of the Spirit (Galatians 5:22-23)?

- How do spiritual gifts relate to offices in the church?

- How do spiritual gifts relate to ministry roles?

Looking Ahead

- At home before the next session, complete the Discover Your Gifts Survey on the next several pages of this book (or online—see survey instructions). The survey will take about 30-45 minutes, and if you do it on paper, you may need extra time to tally the results (see instructions). This survey will help you identify the gifts you have and help you cover important groundwork for the sessions that follow.

Important: You'll be discussing results from your Discover Your Gifts Survey in the next session, so be sure to complete your survey and have results tabulated before then.

- Read section 2 of Part B: FAQs About Spiritual Gifts in this book; the insights there will affirm and build on what you have learned in this session.

Closing

- *Praise* God for the wisdom by which he has made it possible for every believer to engage in ministry.

- *Thank* God for the gifted members of your church. *Give thanks* also that God has given believers talents and fruit and offices and roles, in addition to spiritual gifts.

- *Ask* the Spirit to help you discover your spiritual gifts and help you develop them for service in God's kingdom.

DISCOVER YOUR GIFTS SURVEY

This survey will help you discover your gifts, and we encourage you to confirm them by using them with other Christians in ministry to the glory of God.

Give thanks for the gifts you have been given, and ask the Spirit for guidance in using them. Don't be disappointed if you learn that you do not have some gifts you desire. God may choose to develop those or other gifts in you later. You can trust, though, that God has gifted others in the body of Christ with the gifts you do not have.

Be content and willing to learn from God's distribution of gifts and ministry in the church. Affirm one another and celebrate together the gifts you have. Build each other up by noting how you can see particular gifts in one another as you do ministry together. Thank the Spirit for the wonderful diversity within the body of Christ (Rom. 12:4-5; 1 Cor. 12), knowing that you all benefit each other to the glory of God as you use your gifts.

How to Complete the Survey

You can complete the survey on paper (on the following pages) or online via the Internet. It will take about 30-45 minutes to complete this survey.

To access the survey online, enter the access code provided with this book (printed on the inside back cover) at the website address www.FaithAliveResources.org/DiscoverYourGiftsSurvey, and follow the instructions there. (*Note:* The access code is valid for only one user.)

This survey uses a scale of 0-7 (with 7 as the strongest value) to help you state how strongly each statement describes you. Read each statement and select the number that shows **how strongly you identify with the statement** (how often this is true of you, how deeply this is true of you, and so on).

Work quickly. Be honest in your answers—but don't worry about giving a "wrong" answer; your first impressions are usually correct.

Results (Needed for Next Session)

If you complete the survey on paper, you can tally your results by using the Key Chart on page 31 and following the instructions there.

If you complete the survey online, the results will tally automatically for you, and you'll be able to e-mail your results to the leader of this study or to your church office. You may also want to print out a copy of the results for use in your next session.

You'll need to refer to your survey results in the next session (see "What Are My Spiritual Gifts?" in session 3), and your group leader may want to collect them for reference and ministry follow-up later.

Learn More

Once you've discovered your spiritual gifts, learn more about them in the Gift Studies section of this book. Take time also to learn about other gifts so that you can recognize and appreciate the gifts of others. Remember that the purpose of discovering your gifts is to serve well together as the body of Christ, to the glory of God and his kingdom.

On a scale of 0-7 (with 7 as the strongest value), indicate how strongly each statement describes you.

1   I have a sense for how and when a project or ministry needs to be better organized.

    0   1   2   (3)   4   5   6   7

2   I enjoy expressing myself creatively for God through the arts (music, drama, literature, visual arts, etc.).

    0   (1)   2   3   4   5   6   7

3   I detect phoniness or false teachings in situations where others are swayed and misled.

    0   1   2   (3)   4   5   6   7

4   I am excited at the potential I see in people, and I challenge them to do their best for God.

    0   1   2   (3)   4   5   6   7

5   I share the good news of God's saving love with others and often see positive results.

    0   1   (2)   3   4   5   6   7

6   I understand what Jesus meant when he said mountains could be moved by faith.

    0   1   2   3   (4)   5   6   7

7   I give cheerfully and liberally to support the Lord's work.

    0   1   2   3   4   (5)   6   7

8   A deep compassion for sick or broken people motivates me to pray for their healing.

    0   1   2   3   4   (5)   6   7

9   I welcome guests and do not feel imposed upon by unexpected visitors.

    0   1   2   3   (4)   5   6   7

10 I am sensitive to the prayer needs of others and give them a great deal of prayer support.

    0   1   2   3   (4)   5   6   7

11 God has directly revealed things to me that I could not have known any other way.

    0   1   2   (3)   4   5   6   7

12 I can present the vision for a project in a way that attracts others to get involved.

    0   1   2   (3)   4   5   6   7

13 I effectively help hurting people find relief and restoration.

    0   1   2   **(3)**   4   5   6   7

14 I have seen that God works miracles today.

    0   1   2   3   **(4)**   5   6   7

15 God uses me to build up other Christians by speaking to them of spiritual things.

    0   1   2   **(3)**   4   5   6   7

16 I sense when others need a helping hand, and I am eager to help.

    0   1   2   3   **(4)**   5   6   7

17 My concern for the spiritual well-being of others motivates me to help them grow spiritually.

    0   1   2   **(3)**   4   5   6   7

18 Subject matter comes alive for students (children or adults) when I teach.

    0   **(1)**   2   3   4   5   6   7

19 I have been moved by the Spirit to speak in an unknown language.

  (0)   1   2   3   4   5   6   7

20 I give people practical insights that help them solve problems.

    0   1   2   **(3)**   4   5   6   7

21 I design and carry out effective plans to accomplish goals in ministry.

    0   **(1)**   2   3   4   5   6   7

22 I have communicated biblical truth in artistic ways.

  (0)   1   2   3   4   5   6   7

23 I can tell whether a person's words, actions, or motives are godly, sinful, or from the evil one.

    0   1   2   3   4   **(5)**   6   7

24 I empathize with hurting or discouraged people and want to help them see that they can trust God in all situations.

    0   1   2   **(3)**   4   5   6   7

25 I have helped to lead others to believe in Christ and trust him as Savior.

    0   1   **(2)**   3   4   5   6   7

26 I have known God would intervene supernaturally when it seemed unlikely—and then I saw it happen.

    0   **(1)**   2   3   4   5   6   7

27 I am moved by the Spirit to give when I learn of a need or opportunity.

    0   1   2   3   4   5   **(6)**   7

28 God has used me to help people experience substantial healing in surprising ways.

    0   (1)   2   3   4   5   6   7

29 I enjoy taking care of small details that make a big difference in welcoming guests or strangers.

    0   (1)   2   3   4   5   6   7

30 I identify with and agonize over the needs of others as I pray for them.

    0   1   2   (3)   4   5   6   7

31 I have received thoughts or knowledge directly from the Holy Spirit.

    (0)   1   2   3   4   5   6   7

32 God has used me to motivate others to work together in a ministry or program.

    0   (1)   2   3   4   5   6   7

33 I enjoy helping people who suffer physical, mental, or emotional problems.

    0   (1)   2   3   4   5   6   7

34 God has used me to show his miraculous power in a situation where ordinary means were not sufficient.

    0   (1)   2   3   4   5   6   7

35 I am motivated to declare the truth as God has revealed it to me.

    0   (1)   2   3   4   5   6   7

36 I enjoy doing tasks that help others be more effective in their ministry roles.

    0   (1)   2   3   4   5   6   7

37 I am personally involved in nurturing and discipling ministries.

    (0)   1   2   3   4   5   6   7

38 I communicate truth clearly and effectively so that others learn.

    0   1   (2)   3   4   5   6   7

39 In worship, I have been so caught up in wonder and love for God that I have spoken words I did not understand.

    (0)   1   2   3   4   5   6   7

40 God has given me insights in situations for which there was no previous knowledge.

    (0)   1   2   3   4   5   6   7

41 I am good at motivating, coordinating, and delegating to people involved in a ministry or program.

    0   1   (2)   3   4   5   6   7

42 I have used my ability in music, drama, illustration, or other arts to honor God.

   (0)   1   2   3   4   5   6   7

43 I can see when hidden motives are present in people's words or actions.

   0   1   2   (3)   4   5   6   7

44 I know from experience that counsel and instruction from God's Word will help people grow spiritually.

   0   1   2   3   (4)   5   6   7

45 I care deeply that others do not know Jesus, and I look for opportunities to share the good news of Jesus with them.

   0   1   (2)   3   4   5   6   7

46 God has led me to pray with extraordinary faith that he would accomplish something.

   0   1   2   3   (4)   5   6   7

47 I use money and possessions as tools to show my love for God and others.

   0   1   2   3   4   (5)   6   7

48 I ask God expectantly for healing for persons who are physically, emotionally, or spiritually ill.

   0   1   2   3   4   5   6   (7)

49 I have a knack for making visitors feel at ease in my home or at church.

   0   1   (2)   3   4   5   6   7

50 I am motivated to pray by an inner conviction that God acts in response to my prayers.

   0   1   2   3   4   5   6   (7)

51 I have received God-given, supernatural insights while praying.

   0   1   2   (3)   4   5   6   7

52 I can set goals and find ways to provide what others need to get a project done.

   0   1   2   3   (4)   5   6   7

53 I grieve for people in misery and want to do something to help them.

   0   1   2   3   (4)   5   6   7

54 I sense specific situations in which a miraculous working of God's power would strengthen people's faith in God.

   0   1   (2)   3   4   5   6   7

28   Student Book

55　God has used me to proclaim timely messages that have come to me through his Word and Spirit.

　　0　　(1)　　2　　3　　4　　5　　6　　7

56　I am eager to help others in any kind of work for the church.

　　0　　1　　2　　3　　4　　5　　(6)　　7

57　God has used me to provide ongoing spiritual care and direction for other believers.

　　0　　1　　(2)　　3　　4　　5　　6　　7

58　When I share teachings from the Bible, people listen with interest.

　　0　　(1)　　2　　3　　4　　5　　6　　7

59　I know what God is saying when I hear someone speak in tongues.

　　(0)　　1　　2　　3　　4　　5　　6　　7

60　I am able to apply spiritual understanding in practical ways.

　　0　　(1)　　2　　3　　4　　5　　6　　7

61　I enjoy organizing programs, tasks, and people to achieve an objective for God's kingdom.

　　(0)　　1　　2　　3　　4　　5　　6　　7

62　I am aware that people have been blessed through my creative or artistic ability.

　　(0)　　1　　2　　3　　4　　5　　6　　7

63　I can tell the difference between spiritual truth and error.

　　0　　1　　2　　3　　(4)　　5　　6　　7

64　I give people practical counsel and guidance for their spiritual growth.

　　0　　(1)　　2　　3　　4　　5　　6　　7

65　I am eager to build relationships with non-Christians, hoping I can help them know the Lord.

　　0　　(1)　　2　　3　　4　　5　　6　　7

66　I have trusted and prayed that God would do something despite all kinds of obstacles, and it was accomplished.

　　0　　(1)　　2　　3　　4　　5　　6　　7

67　I make personal sacrifices and avoid getting too deep in debt so I can give for God's work in this world.

　　0　　1　　2　　3　　(4)　　5　　6　　7

68　I like to be involved in ministries or programs that offer care and healing for hurting people.

　　0　　(1)　　2　　3　　4　　5　　6　　7

69 My home is open to people in need of a welcome or a place to stay.

 0 (1) 2 3 4 5 6 7

70 I pray faithfully for others in their work for God, knowing that prayer within God's will is effective.

 0 1 2 3 (4) 5 6 7

71 I have received guidance or insight from the Spirit that has enabled me to help others.

 0 (1) 2 3 4 5 6 7

72 At times, God has given me a sense of vision for a new task or project that attracted others to get involved.

 0 (1) 2 3 4 5 6 7

73 I show kindness and compassion in many ways to all kinds of people.

 0 1 2 (3) 4 5 6 7

74 God has used miraculous power through me to oppose Satan's work.

 (0) 1 2 3 4 5 6 7

75 I am convinced that God wants me to speak out on social and moral issues.

 0 1 2 3 (4) 5 6 7

76 I find practical ways to help others and enjoy doing so.

 0 1 2 3 4 (5) 6 7

77 The Lord uses me to lead and guide other Christians toward spiritual maturity.

 0 1 (2) 3 4 5 6 7

78 I get excited about new or fresh ideas I can share with others.

 0 (1) 2 3 4 5 6 7

79 Believers gathered in worship have been built up by my interpretation of a message spoken in tongues.

 (0) 1 2 3 4 5 6 7

80 God gives me unusually helpful insight into difficult situations.

 0 (1) 2 3 4 5 6 7

KEY CHART

How to Use the Key Chart

Fill out the key chart on the next page after completing the survey.

1. In the space next to each number in the key chart, enter the score (0-7) that you assigned to each of the 80 statements in the survey.

2. Add up the four scores in each row, and enter the total in the far-right column.

3. Circle the four highest scores listed in the Total column. These are your four strongest spiritual gifts.

4. Write the names of these four gifts in the blanks at the bottom of the page, listing them from highest scored to lowest. In case of a tie, give a higher rating to the gift that you sense is more dominant. Remember that although the remaining gifts may not be your strongest spiritual gifts, you still have a responsibility in each gift area. God is likely developing additional gifts in you, and God may have plans to empower you with a particular gift in the future.

5. Hand in or send your results to your group leader or gifts administrator. You may want to use the Ready to Serve! form (p. 126) for this purpose. We recommend that you take this survey again periodically (every 3-5 years) to update how God is developing you to serve as an increasingly gifted member of his kingdom.

Key Chart

Spiritual Gift	Responses				Total
Administration	1 _3_	21 _/_	41 _2_	61 _0_	_6_
Creative Ability	2 _/_	22 _0_	42 _0_	62 _0_	_/_
Discernment	3 _3_	23 _5_	43 _3_	63 _4_	_15_
Encouragement	4 _3_	24 _3_	44 _4_	64 _/_	_11_
Evangelism	5 _2_	25 _2_	45 _2_	65 _/_	_7_
Faith	6 _4_	26 _/_	46 _4_	66 _/_	_10_
Giving	7 _5_	27 _6_	47 _5_	67 _4_	_20_
Healing	8 _5_	28 _/_	48 _7_	68 _/_	_11_
Hospitality	9 _4_	29 _/_	49 _2_	69 _/_	_8_
Intercession	10 _4_	30 _3_	50 _7_	70 _4_	_18_
Knowledge	11 _3_	31 _0_	51 _3_	71 _/_	_7_
Leadership	12 _3_	32 _/_	52 _4_	72 _/_	_9_
Mercy	13 _3_	33 _/_	53 _4_	73 _3_	_11_
Miracles	14 _4_	34 _/_	54 _2_	74 _0_	_7_
Prophecy	15 _3_	35 _/_	55 _/_	75 _4_	_9_
Service (Helping)	16 _4_	36 _0_	56 _6_	76 _5_	_15_
Shepherding (Pastoring)	17 _3_	37 _2_	57 _2_	77 _2_	_9_
Teaching	18 _/_	38 _0_	58 _/_	78 _/_	_3_
Tongues (Speaking and Interpretation)	19 _0_	39 _0_	59 _0_	79 _0_	_0_
Wisdom	20 _3_	40 _0_	60 _/_	80 _/_	_5_

My Gifts

Highest scored gift _Giving_

2nd _Intercession_

3rd _Service_

4th _Discernment_

CONFIRMING MY SPIRITUAL GIFTS

Opening Prayer

Preview

In this session we will

- define and explain several more spiritual gifts.

- learn that gifts have both natural and supernatural components.

- learn how we can confirm our own spiritual gifts.

What Are My Spiritual Gifts?

In small groups of three or four persons, name your top gifts as identified in the Discover Your Gifts Survey; then comment on one or both of these questions:

- Did the survey results surprise you at all? Explain.

- Do your interests line up with these gifts? Explain.

Pick one of your top gifts and respond to these questions:

- Have you have already used this gift in some way? (In other words, does your experience confirm this gift?) If so, how?

- How might God want you to use this gift in the future?

Bible Discovery

In this session we will continue our study of spiritual gifts by focusing on gifts mentioned in 1 Corinthians 12. Again, while the gifts highlighted in this course are those most commonly found in Scripture, others may be identified, and other names for the gifts may be used.

Wisdom

The Spirit-given ability to see situations and issues from God's perspective and to apply God-given insights to specific areas of need.

1 Corinthians 12:8—*To one there is given through the Spirit a message of wisdom. . . .*

- The basic idea of this gift is . . .

- Do you know (or know of) someone who has this gift? If so, who?

Knowledge

The Spirit-given ability to receive from God knowledge that is crucial to ministry and that could not have been obtained in other ways.

1 Corinthians 12:8—*To another [is given] a message of knowledge by means of the same Spirit. . . .*

- The basic idea of this gift is . . .

- Do you know (or know of) someone who has this gift? If so, who?

Faith

The Spirit-given ability to know that God wills to do something, even when there is no concrete evidence to support that conviction.

1 Corinthians 12:9—*To another [is given] faith by the same Spirit. . . .*

- The basic idea of this gift is . . .

- Do you know (or know of) someone who has this gift? If so, who?

Healing
The Spirit-given ability to serve as an instrument through whom God brings physical, emotional, and spiritual healing in both ordinary and extraordinary ways.

1 Corinthians 12:9—*To another [is given] gifts of healing by that one Spirit. . . .*

- The basic idea of this gift is . . .

- Do you know (or know of) someone who has this gift? If so, who?

Miracles
The Spirit-given ability to serve as an instrument through whom God performs extraordinary works as an expression of his presence and power.

1 Corinthians 12:10—*To another [is given] miraculous powers. . . .*

- The basic idea of this gift is . . .

- Do you know (or know of) someone who has this gift? If so, who?

Discernment
The Spirit-given ability to know whether a statement, action, or motive has its source in God, our sinful human nature, or Satan.

1 Corinthians 12:10—*To another [is given the gift of] distinguishing between spirits. . . .*

- The basic idea of this gift is . . .

- Do you know (or know of) someone who has this gift? If so, who?

Tongues (Speaking and Interpretation)
The Spirit-given ability to speak in a language previously unknown to the speaker and/or to interpret for the benefit of the church.

1 Corinthians 12:10—*To another [is given the gift of] speaking in different kinds of tongues, and to still another the interpretation of tongues.*

- The basic idea of this gift is . . .

- Do you know (or know of) someone who has this gift? If so, who?

Natural and Supernatural

All gifts are empowered by the Spirit. With some gifts the power may seem to be mostly *natural,* within our normal experience. With other gifts the power may appear to be mostly *supernatural,* beyond our normal experience. All gifts have some degree of both the natural and supernatural, however. The degrees to which they are natural and supernatural vary from gift to gift.

- Gifts that seem to be mostly natural: mercy, service, teaching, encouragement, giving, leadership, administration

- Gifts that seem to be mostly supernatural: healing, miracles, tongues

- Would you describe the following gifts as mostly natural or mostly supernatural? (Don't be concerned about giving "right" or "wrong" answers; remember that all spiritual gifts are somewhat natural and somewhat supernatural.)

    —wisdom

    —discernment

    —prophecy

    —knowledge

    —faith

    —evangelism

    —shepherding

    —creative ability

    —hospitality

    —intercession

Acknowledge together that it is not always possible to know whether our use of gifts depends on the natural or the supernatural. For example, discernment can be very natural. There are some very discerning people.

On the other hand, the Holy Spirit can supernaturally give a person the discernment that would help a church guard against false teachers and false teachings. The gifts of wisdom and knowledge could be described similarly.

The words of Scripture do not draw a line to distinguish between natural and supernatural aspects of the Spirit's gifts. It's best to recognize that there's ambiguity here and to encourage one another to look for evidence of natural and supernatural aspects of gifts in our own living for God and his kingdom.

How to Confirm Your Spiritual Gifts

The following points outline important steps you can take to confirm your spiritual gifts.

1. Understand the gifts.

The Gift Studies section (Part C) of this book will help you understand and confirm your spiritual gifts. Study these on your own and be prepared to share insights you have gained when you meet for your next session.

2. Accept the fact that you are gifted.

The Bible speaks of each believer as having gifts. So if you are a believer, you have gifts. Say to someone else in your class, "I think the Holy Spirit has given me these gifts: _____ _____
_____.
I have these gifts from God so that I can use them for the good of others."
Don't be afraid to say this to others in or outside of class.

3. Analyze yourself.

Assume that God is already at work in you and through you. Try to confirm your gifts by looking at what God is doing in your life. Take a few minutes to ask yourself the following questions about skills and interests. These can help you see areas in which you can use your gifts.

(To help you get started, here are some examples of interests and skills: music, carpentry, math, sewing, art, cooking, computer programming, landscaping, medicine, counseling, writing, auto mechanics, engineering, accounting, law, public relations, advertising, journalism, aerobics, painting, electrical work, library, drama, sound systems, multimedia, building maintenance, coaching, typing, science, history, religion, literature, sports, psychology.)

- What are my interests?

- What have I done well in the past?

- What do I really get excited about doing?
- What needs am I most aware of in my church and/or community?

4. Pray.
Thank God for your gifts. *Submit* them to God. *Ask* for guidance. (You'll have an opportunity to pray privately at the end of this session.)

Here's a sample prayer: "Father, I thank you for the spiritual gifts you have given me by your Holy Spirit. Confirm in my life what *you know* my gifts to be. I am willing to use them as you want me to so that your name will be glorified. Guide me to ministries that make a difference in your kingdom. I really want to serve you! In Jesus' name, Amen."

5. Seek confirmation from other Christians.
Listen for affirming comments from other believers engaged in ministry. Those who know you best, such as family members and close friends, will often be the first to notice and point out what you do well. Give others confirming feedback when you see them doing things well.

6. Get involved in ministry.
You will never know your abilities until you begin to act.

7. Evaluate the results.
If you are using your gifts in ministry, you should soon begin to see confirming results.

Looking Ahead

- In the Gift Studies section (Part C) of this book, study the top four gifts you have identified as your spiritual gifts. From your study and from your own experience with these gifts, be prepared to share in a discussion during the next session.

- Read section 3 of Part B: FAQs About Spiritual Gifts in this book; the insights there will affirm and expand on what you have learned in this session.

Closing

- In a time of individual silent prayer you can offer your own version of a prayer of thanks, submission, and asking of God (see suggestion in point 4 above).

- Sing together "Spirit of the Living God." Make it your communal prayer. Be especially mindful of God's work in you as you sing the words "use me."

THE SPIRITUALLY GIFTED CHURCH

Opening Prayer

Preview

In this session we will

- see how spiritual gifts are meant to benefit the church.

- note how gifts can be misused in the church.

- observe a distinction between working gifts and waiting gifts.

What I Have Learned About My Gifts

In a small group with three or four others, take about three minutes each to share the most important things you have learned about one of your gifts from the Gift Studies in Part C of this book. For example,

- Explain the gift in your own words.

- Describe the characteristics of a person who has this gift. (This could be a person mentioned in the Bible, an imaginary person, or yourself.)

- Explain how the gift can work well in one-on-one relationships, in the church, or in the broader community, and how you use or would like to use this gift.

Depending on how well you know each other, affirm one another in the use of the gifts people have mentioned in your group.

Bible Discovery

Read the following Bible passages and answer the accompanying questions. Note that the apostle Paul always places his discussion of spiritual gifts within the context of the body of Christ—that is, the church. In this exercise we'll explore how our gifts benefit the church and how they can be misused and cause problems for the church.

How Our Gifts Benefit the Church

Romans 12:4-5

4For just as each of us has one body with many members, and these members do not all have the same function, 5so in Christ we who are many form one body, and each member belongs to all the others.

- How does a body with many different parts work best?

  work together

- What does it mean to belong to one another?

  to support

1 Corinthians 12:25-26

25. . . There should be no division in the body, but . . . its parts should have equal concern for each other. 26If one part suffers, every part suffers with it; if one part is honored, every part rejoices with it.

- How should the many parts (members) of the gifted church interact with each other?

  support each other

- How does this benefit the body of Christ as a whole?

  a house divided will fall

Ephesians 4:11-13

11So Christ himself gave the apostles, the prophets, the evangelists, the pastors and teachers, 12to equip his people for works of service, so that the body of Christ may be built up 13until we all reach unity in the faith and in the knowledge of the Son of God and become mature, attaining to the whole measure of the fullness of Christ.

- How does the church benefit as spiritually gifted leaders use their gifts?

1 Corinthians 14:3-4

3But those who prophesy speak to people for their strengthening, encouragement and comfort. 4Those who speak in a tongue edify [help, build up] themselves, but those who prophesy edify the church.

- What does this passage say about the purpose of gifts?

  They should to used to build the church.

How Gifts Can Be Misused

1 Corinthians 12:14-16, 21

14Even so the body is not made up of one part but of many. 15Now if the foot should say, "Because I am not a hand, I do not belong to the body," it would not for that reason cease to be part of the body. 16And if the ear should say, "Because I am not an eye, I do not belong to the body," it would not for that reason cease to be part of the body. . . .

21The eye cannot say to the hand, "I don't need you!" And the head cannot say to the feet, "I don't need you!"

- What problem is pictured in this passage?

- What do you think the solution would be?

1 Corinthians 12:27-30

27Now you are the body of Christ, and each one of you is a part of it. 28And God has placed in the church first of all apostles, second prophets, third teachers, then miracles, then gifts of healing, of helping, of guidance, and of different kinds of tongues. 29Are all apostles? Are all prophets? Are all teachers? Do all work miracles? 30Do all have gifts of healing? Do all speak in tongues? Do all interpret?

- What misuse of gifts is implied here?

- How might this problem be corrected?

1 Corinthians 13:1-3

1If I speak in human or angelic tongues, but do not have love, I am only a resounding gong or a clanging cymbal. 2If I have the gift of prophecy and can fathom all mysteries and all knowledge, and if I have a faith that can move mountains, but do not have love, I am nothing. 3If I give all I possess to the poor and give over my body to hardship that I may boast, but do not have love, I gain nothing.

- What's the potential problem described here?

- What is the simple but important solution?

  love

- What practical difference will love make as you use your gifts?

  correct

1 Corinthians 14:26-28, 40

[26]*What then shall we say, brothers and sisters? When you come together, each of you has a hymn, or a word of instruction, a revelation, a tongue or an interpretation. Everything must be done so that the church may be built up.* [27]*If anyone speaks in a tongue, two—or at the most three—should speak, one at a time, and someone must interpret.* [28]*If there is no interpreter, the speaker should keep quiet in the church; let them speak to themselves and to God. . . .*

[40]*But everything should be done in a fitting and orderly way.*

- What problems is the writer urging people to avoid here?

  disorder

- How can these problems be avoided?

Pulling Our Thoughts Together

Howard Snyder in *The Problem of Wineskins* writes,

> The church truly becomes the church only when the biblical meaning of spiritual gifts is recovered. A church whose life and ministry is not built upon the exercise of spiritual gifts is biblically a contradiction in terms.

With Snyder's quote in mind, consider the following questions:

1. Are the benefits identified in the Bible passages above still present in the church today? Are any of the problems still present? Do Paul's solutions still apply? Explain.

2. What new or different problems about gifts are you aware of in today's church? What solutions would you propose?

3. If a church's life and ministry are built on gifts, how will that affect the church's various ministries? Its organizational structure?

    build on its strength

4. What action would you like to see your church take regarding spiritual gifts and ministries?

    more people involved

Working Gifts and Waiting Gifts

In the Discover Your Gifts Survey, you identified gifts that you are already using or have the strongest potential to use in ministry for the kingdom of God. These are commonly referred to as your *working gifts*. A working gift is a spiritual gift you are aware of because you have used it. It's working.

By comparison, a *waiting gift* is a gift that you may have the potential for developing. You may not be aware of this gift yet, perhaps because you have not used it or God hasn't given you the occasion to use or develop it yet. It's waiting to be identified and developed. Waiting gifts can often be discovered by looking into your interests, inclinations, sensitivities, and concerns.

It's important to know at least some of your waiting gifts. As we grow more mature in Christ, God may shape us for ministries that we were not capable to do earlier. As we grow older, the Spirit may give us gifts that match our diminishing energy levels. In addition, a move to a new community or a new church may open doors to new ministry opportunities.

Look together at the Waiting Gifts Survey (in Part D of this book) and plan on filling this out before your next session. The survey will take about 15-20 minutes to complete.

Looking Ahead

- Between this session and the next, complete the Waiting Gifts Survey found in Part D of this book. It will help you identify potential gifts that God may develop in you later. Be ready to report on your results in the next session (see "What Are My Waiting Gifts?" in session 5).

- Continue studying your spiritual gifts in Part C: Gift Studies, especially waiting gifts you have identified in the Waiting Gifts Survey. You'll be able to share more about your gifts with a small group during your next session. Go on to study the gifts other people have as well.

- Read the FAQs About Spiritual Gifts that connect with this session (see Part B, section 4, in this book). The insights there will affirm and build on what you have learned in this session.

Closing Prayer

- *Praise* the Holy Spirit for empowering the members of the body of Christ each day.

- *Thank* God for the gifted community of which you are a part. Think back through experiences in the church and recall with gratitude to

God the many times and ways in which gifted people have been a blessing to you.

- *Confess* for yourself and/or for your church any problematic behaviors related to gifts.

- *Ask* God for continued strength and courage as you seek to use your gifts together to build up the church, doing the work of God's kingdom today.

USING MY SPIRITUAL GIFTS FOR MINSTRY

Opening Prayer

Preview

In this session we will

- learn that the Holy Spirit is God's agent of empowerment.

- discover and reflect more on the link between spiritual gifts and ministry.

- learn how our passions for ministry relate to our spiritual gifts.

What Are My Waiting Gifts?

In small groups of three or four persons, each one of you can name your waiting gifts as identified in the Waiting Gifts Survey (completed before this session). Then comment on one or two of these questions:

- Were you surprised by what you discovered? Explain.

- Does your current experience confirm these gifts in some way? Explain.

- How might God want you to use these gifts in the future?

Bible Discovery

Read the following Bible passages and answer the discovery questions that follow.

Empowered for Ministry

Acts 1:8
"You will receive power when the Holy Spirit comes on you; and you will be my witnesses in Jerusalem, and in all Judea and Samaria, and to the ends of the earth."

1 Corinthians 12:7
To each one . . . [gifts are] given for the common good.

Ephesians 4:11-12
Christ himself gave . . . [gifts] to equip his people for works of service, so that the body of Christ may be built up.

1 Peter 4:10
Each of you should use whatever gift you have received to serve others, as faithful stewards of God's grace. . . .

- What is essential for effective ministry? Where does it come from?

  Holy Spirit work in us.

- According to these passages, what are God's reasons for giving gifts? (You'll find at least three here, and you may be able to think of more.)

  so we may witness & build up the church & common good.

- How does the church benefit if gifts are used as God has intended?

  build up. enrich

Gifts and Ministry Passions

God has given you particular spiritual gifts that uniquely equip you for service. God has probably also given you a desire to make a difference in a particular ministry area. For example, it may be a concern for a specific human need in an area that interests you. This may be your ministry passion.

Your ministry passion is something that you care deeply about, something that drives you. Your passion will pull you toward a particular area of ministry. You will be most effective and fulfilled in ministry if you use spiritual gifts in an area where you have a strong desire to make a difference.

In order to find clues to your ministry passion, you need to think about what most interests you. What do you get really excited about learning or doing? What do you think are the most important problems that need to be addressed? The following exercise is designed to help you discover your ministry passions.

Take a few minutes to work through the following questions, marking items that apply to you. Your responses here can help you gain a sense of your ministry passions in connection with the spiritual gifts you have.

Finding Out My Ministry Passions

1. Which of the following groups of people do I most like working with? Which of these am I most concerned about?

    ____ Infants __✓__ Children ____ Teens ____ Young adults

    __✓__ Adults ____ Singles ____ Couples ____ Elderly ___ Other

2. In which of the following areas do I have the strongest feeling that things should be changed? (This is not an exhaustive list but simply an attempt to stimulate thinking.)

    __✓__ Poverty __✓__ Hunger ____ Ecological issues

    ____ Crime ____ Drug/Alcohol abuse ____ Illiteracy

    ____ Health care ____ Physical disabilities

    ____ Doctrinal issues ____ AIDS ____ Emotional distress

    ____ Ethical issues ____ Crisis pregnancies

    ____ Care of senior citizens ____ Learning disabilities

    ____ Family problems ____ Generation gaps

    ____ Spiritual lostness ____ Spiritual immaturity

    ____ Other:

3. Which of the following ministry areas am I most interested in?

    ____ Worship ____ Education/Discipling ____ Evangelism

    __✓__ Caring ____ Enfolding ____ Communications/Marketing

    ____ Fundraising __✓__ Stewardship ___ World Missions

—This material is adapted from an unpublished gift-discovery course developed by David Armstrong, Kevin Blair, Robert Boomsma, Barbara Brouwer, Brenda Cook, Karen Folkerts, and Judy Stremler of Elmhurst Christian Reformed Church, Elmhurst, Illinois. Used by permission.

You'll want to spend time reflecting at home on how your responses to this exercise connect to your spiritual gifts and how you can use them in areas of ministry that you are passionate about. You can also include your reflections on the Ready to Serve! form (in Part D of this book), which you can hand in to your leader or submit to your church office after completing this course.

My Action Plan

Work individually to answer the following questions:

- Considering the gifts God has given me, what does the Lord want me to do for him . . .

   —in my relationships with family, friends, or coworkers?

   —in my church? *go on mission trips*

   —in the broader community?
   help people — disater releaf

- What will help me do these things? What might hinder me?

- How might I be able to use my gifts more fully? (Be as specific as possible.)

Share your plan with others in a small group; then be ready to offer comments when you regather as a whole class.

Looking Ahead

- Spend some more time at home reflecting on your ministry passions and how they can help give direction to your use of spiritual gifts.

- Complete the Ready to Serve! form in Part D of this book and provide a copy for your leader.

- Read and reflect on the FAQs About Spiritual Gifts connected with this session (Part B, section 5), and follow up with a self-study of all the spiritual gifts covered in Part C of this book. Learn how all these spiritual gifts can be used in the body of Christ—and discover how they can work in connection with the gifts you have.

Closing

Close this final session together with a commissioning of all participants to use the gifts God has given you for ministry. A sample commissioning litany follows on the next page.

COMMISSIONING LITANY

Leader: God commands us, as members of the body of Christ: "Each of you should use whatever gift you have received to serve others, as faithful stewards of God's grace in its various forms"; you are called to serve God with your gifts "so that in all things God may be praised through Jesus Christ" (1 Pet. 4:10-11).

Now that you know your spiritual gifts, you are called to be fruitfully engaged with the people of God in building up the body of Christ. Through its spiritually gifted members the church provides opportunities for believers to build each other up; encourages the people of God as they care for others in need; and reaches out to people who are yet without faith and hope in God.

As you step into the ministries for which God has prepared and called you, please answer the following questions:

- Do you believe that God will guide you in using your spiritual gifts for his glory, to build up the church, the body of Christ, and to advance the kingdom of God?

- Do you promise to develop your spiritual gifts and to use them for the Lord by lovingly serving others?

Response
All: We do, with God's help!

Encouragement
Leader: Servants of God, let us rejoice that the Lord has gifted you and called you to serve in many different ways. Serving the Lord Jesus is a high calling and a great privilege. Carry out your callings with distinction and find great joy in your service. By the Father's grace in Christ may you be enlightened and strengthened by the Holy Spirit to serve faithfully and fruitfully to the glory of God.

Prayer
Leader: Father, give each of these gifted servants a fresh anointing of your Spirit so that they may have the words and the strength to serve you well. Open for them doors of opportunity to serve, and fill them to overflowing so that your love will flow through them like living water to all whose lives are touched by their ministries.

All: We pray in the name of the triune God who gives us gifts and empowers us to use them. Amen.

FAQs ABOUT SPIRITUAL GIFTS

FAQs ABOUT SPIRITUAL GIFTS

Section 1

1. Why study spiritual gifts?

There are several good reasons to study spiritual gifts:

- **First, it's a matter of obedience.** The apostle Paul says, "Now about the gifts of the Spirit, brothers and sisters, I do not want you to be uninformed" (1 Cor. 12:1).

- **Second, the church will benefit and its ministries will become increasingly effective** as its members discover and use their gifts. God intends the church to capitalize on the strengths of its members.

- **Third, individual believers will mature in their self-image and faith** as they sense the competence God has given them. They will also excel in ministry and find fulfillment by ministering out of their spiritual strengths.

2. What are spiritual gifts?

Spiritual gifts are special abilities given by Christ through the Holy Spirit to empower believers for the ministries of the body.

Let's look at each phrase in this definition:

- **special abilities**—These are abilities that exceed the normal ability level of others in the church. By such abilities believers are able to do something well for the Lord, making a distinctive contribution for the well-being of the whole. Believers often find that their gifts are similar to or complement natural talents they have. Sometimes, however, these abilities are radically new and different from abilities and talents a person had before coming to faith in Christ.

- **given by Christ**—Christ, ruling from his throne in heaven, continues to be active in this world, exercising his lordship in and through believers by providing them with unique gifts for ministry. With these gifts believers accomplish God's work on earth, help build God's kingdom, and exercise God's authority over powers of darkness.

- **through the Holy Spirit**—The Holy Spirit, working with the Father and the Son (see 1 Cor. 12:4-11), provides the motivation, energy, and guidance that operates within the gifted person. The Spirit is able to operate this way from his place within the heart of every believer. The Spirit moves in response to our asking and our faithful obedience.

- **to empower believers**—Power from the Holy Spirit translates into a strength or competency that causes the gifted person to act for the purpose of advancing the kingdom of God.

- **for the ministries of the body**—Gifts are given so that believers can engage in ministries that build up the church (the body of Christ) and advance Christ's kingdom in the world.

3. Why are spiritual gifts given?
The Holy Spirit gives spiritual gifts for at least three reasons:

- that Christians may minister to each other in the body of Christ. The apostle Paul states that gifts are given "for the common good" (1 Cor. 12:7). The apostle Peter says we ought to use our gifts "to serve others" (1 Pet. 4:10).

- "that the body of Christ may be built up"—that is, grow in unity and maturity in Christ (Eph. 4:11-16). As believers use their gifts, the church's witness and ministry are extended in the world.

- that God may be glorified. Peter observes that God will be glorified in everything if believers, exercising their gifts, speak the words of God and serve in the strength that God supplies (1 Pet. 4:11).

Believers receive affirmation as they learn that their gifts are useful in service to the Master. Believers' sense of belonging to Christ and his church is also strengthened as they use their gifts together.

4. What are the benefits of knowing our spiritual gifts?
We can identify several benefits:

- Knowing our gifts can assist us in finding God's will for our lives. Discovering gifts will uncover our spiritual job description. Once we have identified our gifts, we will be able to concentrate on what God has intended us to do. In *Eighth Day of Creation*, Elizabeth O'Connor writes, "When one really becomes practical about gifts, they spell out responsibility and sacrifice. . . . The identifying of gifts brings to the fore . . . the issue of commitment. Somehow, if I name my gift and it is confirmed, I cannot 'hang loose' in the same way. . . . I must give up being a straddler. . . ."

• Knowing our gifts can help us overcome feelings of inadequacy and inferiority. Each of us is important to the church. Every believer has a God-given mission. There are no second-class citizens in God's kingdom.

• By knowing our gifts, we can be more effective in service. We are most effective and productive when we are doing what God has equipped us to do. We are enabled to be channels of God's grace.

• In Romans 12:5 Paul writes, "Each member belongs to all the others." God has given us a place in his body on earth. We are not meant to stand alone or to function apart from the support of the Christian community.

• We are free not to serve in areas where we are not particularly gifted. Knowing our gifts may help us to say no without feeling guilty if we are asked to do things beyond our giftedness. God does not want us to race from one ministry activity to the next, regardless of our giftedness.

5. Are there spiritual gifts not mentioned in the New Testament?
Many significant abilities being used in ministries today are not specifically mentioned in the New Testament as spiritual gifts. Believers who are involved in defending the faith; leading in worship; fund-raising; providing Christian medical, psychological, and social care; working with people who have cognitive impairments; foster parenting; performing or directing in the fine arts, such as music, dance, drama, storytelling; public speaking; and much more are exercising many aspects of spiritual giftedness if they're using them in the Lord's service.

Some of these may just be contemporary names for spiritual gifts that are actually listed in the New Testament. Others may be ministries that are possible because of a particular combination of gifts. Still others may be actual gifts that differ from anything mentioned in the Bible's passages on gifts. The array of gifts in the New Testament reflects life in the early church. Since that time the Holy Spirit has continued to empower believers for service in a rich variety of ways.

6. Are some gifts mentioned in the Bible no longer valid?
According to some biblical scholars, certain spiritual gifts were necessary to lay the foundations of the early church but are no longer operative. Gifts

such as apostleship, prophecy, tongues, healing, and miracles are often thought to be in this category.

Other scholars find no warrant from Scripture to say that the use of any gift has ceased. They argue that the Holy Spirit is free to use whatever gifts may suit God's purposes in any age. In *Community of the King,* Howard Snyder writes, "The question is whether the Spirit still gives gifts . . . and the answer is yes. Precisely which gifts [are given] in any particular age is God's prerogative, and we should not prejudge God."

As the church, we can begin by discovering, developing, and using gifts that are currently acknowledged and needed for ministries. Let us also recognize the Lord's freedom to give gifts according to his will, and let us be open to the full spectrum of gifts for the life of the church and the spread of God's kingdom in this world.

Section 2

7. Can a person have more than one spiritual gift?

Most Christians, if not all, have more than one spiritual gift. In fact, most of us have many gifts. While we may have one gift that is more prominent than others, we should recognize that God wants to develop gifts in us so that we can all serve in many ways together as the body of Christ. God's goal for us in Christ is to make us more and more like Christ as we grow to maturity in faith (Rom. 8:29; 2 Cor. 3:18; Eph. 4:13).

A combination of spiritual gifts given to a Christian is called a *gift mix*. A person's gift mix will usually help point out a ministry direction. A person with the gifts of mercy, leadership, and administration, for example, will make a good director of a compassion-oriented ministry. A person whose gift mix is hospitality, mercy, and encouragement will do well in helping a displaced family find a place to live and get resettled. A person who has gifts of evangelism and teaching will be an effective leader of an evangelistic Bible study group.

8. Are all gifts equal?

The Bible does not classify specific gifts as "greater" or "lesser." It points to the rich variety of gifts that the Spirit gives the people of God. Every gift is important in the body of Christ. All gifts are interrelated, and none functions well in isolation from the others. That each member has been given different gifts or a unique gift mix calls for rejoicing.

The words of 1 Corinthians 12:31—"Now eagerly desire the greater gifts"— suggest that some gifts are more important than others. But both the verb and the object in this sentence are plural. So the mandate is directed not to individual Christians but to the church in general. The church communally, not individually, should desire the gifts that will help build it, not simply those that may be most visible.

9. How do spiritual gifts differ from natural talents?

Spiritual gifts and natural talents are alike in several ways. Both are given by God. Both are possessed by believers. Both can be used for the glory of God. But they are not the same. When the apostle Paul describes spiritual gifts, he is speaking of abilities given specifically for building up the church and advancing the kingdom of Christ.

Gifts and talents are often finely interwoven within the same person. In the book *I Believe in the Holy Spirit*, Michael Green writes,

> The charismatic gifts are nothing other than the gifts of God's love. They begin with our redemption. They include the heightening of qualities already present or latent within us, such as the gift of administration, leadership, teaching, marriage, or celibacy. These natural qualities can be charismata [spiritual gifts] if, and so long as, they are dedicated to the service of the Lord and the building up of his people in the strength that he gives. If they are used selfishly, they can be disastrous.

Donald Clifton and Marcus Buckingham in their signature book on strengths define talents as "any recurring pattern of thought, feeling, or behavior that can be productively applied" (*Now, Discover Your Strengths*). What they describe as a talent is something innate to human beings. Spiritual gifts, however, go beyond the innate. The Holy Spirit within each believer, often beginning with the innate natural talent, heightens the natural strength in order to enhance it for kingdom purposes.

10. How are spiritual gifts different from the fruit of the Spirit?

The fruit of the Spirit is meant to be part of every Christian's life. Compare, for example, Galatians 5:22-23 and 1 Corinthians 13:4-7, both of which describe the life of the believer in connection with the love of God. Many other passages describe aspects of Christian living that can be called fruit of the Spirit as well.

Spiritual gifts are Spirit-given abilities for service in the kingdom of God. While each Christian's life should produce *all* kinds of spiritual fruit, each Christian is given only *some* spiritual gifts.

11. How do spiritual gifts differ from offices in the church?

Offices in the church such as minister, elder, and deacon are positions to which the church elects and ordains some gifted members for the purpose of performing official ministries. These offices serve to build up the people of God and help believers remain in fellowship with their Lord. In addition, officebearers help spiritually gifted members function effectively in ministry. They train members to develop their gifts (see Eph. 4:12).

While the offices of the church belong to some members; spiritual gifts belong to all. In some circles the responsibility of all believers to serve is called the office of the believer.

No essential difference exists between the ministries of gifted members of the church and the ministries of officebearers. All Christians minister by means of spiritual gifts. All represent Christ, and all function with some measure of Christ's power and authority.

12. What is the difference between a spiritual gift and a ministry role?
In many cases the Bible commands us all to do what the spiritually gifted person is doing when using a gift. All Christians are to give generously, to be merciful, to have faith, to pray, and so on. We are called to do these to the best of our ability. Some Christians, however, have extraordinary abilities when it comes to giving, mercy, faith, and intercession. These extraordinary abilities are what the Bible calls spiritual gifts.

It is helpful to distinguish, as Peter Wagner does, between spiritual gifts and roles. If one has a spiritual gift, he or she is called to exercise that gift to a greater-than-average degree. For example, if a person has the gift of intercession, that person is challenged to spend more time in prayer than most fellow believers. But all have the *role* of intercession and should therefore pray for others and the working of God's purpose in their lives as the Spirit leads them to. A person with the gift of mercy is called to engage in a ministry of mercy; others, however, are still called to show mercy as it applies in whatever ministry they are involved in. For them, mercy is a role.

13. Do we keep the same spiritual gifts all our lives?
Gifts are an integral part of who we are. Ordinarily they are lifetime trusts. It is possible, however, for gifts to become dormant if they are not developed and used. Paul reminds Timothy, "Do not neglect your gift" (1 Tim. 4:14), and later he challenges Timothy to "fan into flame the gift of God, which is in you" (2 Tim. 1:6). As we move from one situation to another in our lives, a gift may be temporarily deemphasized if opportunities to use it are not readily available. This doesn't mean, however, that the gift is lost.

It may also happen that as the Lord leads a person into new situations, the Spirit awakens spiritual gifts of which the person was previously unaware. For example, this can happen to parents whose children grow up and leave home. Their decreased responsibilities for childcare may open up new possibilities for service. An active person who has been paralyzed in an accident may begin to use a latent gift that doesn't require mobility. We should be open at all times to the Holy Spirit's call to new ministries that require gifts we may not have used or developed before.

Section 3

14. How many spiritual gifts are there?

The Bible does not establish a definite number of spiritual gifts. While some gifts are identified fairly clearly, some important gifts that we can use to build up the body of Christ may be implied or simply not mentioned in the Scriptures. In addition, the words Paul uses to identify gifts do not always identify clear categories. It is difficult to know, for example, whether a gift such as "a message of knowledge" (1 Cor. 12:8) is the same as or different from the gift of teaching (Rom. 12:7; 1 Cor. 12:28-29). We simply don't know for sure. Some Scripture passages list various gifts, but there is nothing to suggest that the total of those provides a complete list of the Spirit's gifts. It is probably best to regard every Spirit-given, Spirit-directed, and Spirit-empowered ability that is used for building up the body of Christ as a spiritual gift, regardless of what we might name it.

15. How do the natural and supernatural combine in spiritual gifts?

Some gifts, like teaching or leadership, seem to be mainly natural abilities. On the other hand, gifts like tongues or healing may seem more supernatural. The truth is that *all* spiritual gifts have a natural and a supernatural dimension. But the balance in each case may be different— shifted toward the natural or toward the supernatural.

For example, a naturally gifted *teacher* who becomes a Christian and receives the spiritual gift of teaching will find his or her natural abilities supernaturally enhanced as the Holy Spirit gives insights into how to clarify, illustrate, and apply the material to be taught. The teacher may also have Spirit-given insights into the learning capabilities of various students. A person with the spiritual gift of *healing*, which sometimes involves remarkable supernatural power, may also have a natural inclination to be sensitive to persons with emotional, physical, or spiritual maladies. The gifted *prophet* may receive messages from God through the Spirit. That's obviously supernatural. Or God may speak to this person through the Bible. That seems more natural and connected with study and scholarship. And yet this person may deliver the message from God with a voice, a presence, and a power that is rooted in the natural and enhanced by the Holy Spirit.

16. What hinders Christians from discovering their spiritual gifts?

A number of things may hinder a Christian from discovering his or her spiritual gifts:

- **Lack of ministry experience.** Christians often discover that they have a spiritual gift when they experience success in a particular ministry. People who are not involved in ministry will not have this opportunity for gift discovery. For this reason new converts, who have little or no experience in ministering, may have more difficulty discovering their gifts. New converts and others with little ministry experience are able, however, to discover gifts that they have a potential for developing. In this course we call those gifts *waiting gifts*, and a person discovers them by carefully monitoring his or her abilities, desires, interests, and inclinations.

- **Disobedience.** Obedience leads to discovery of gifts. The disobedience of not taking one's place of service in the church may hinder discovery.

- **An unloving spirit.** Gift ministries must always be ministries of love. According to the apostle Paul, gifts and ministries without love are worth nothing (1 Cor. 13:1-3). If we seek to discover gifts without the motive of love, even our seeking will be hindered.

- **Lack of prayer.** James chided early Christians whose desires were not fulfilled: "You do not have, because you do not ask God" (James 4:2). God is committed to answering when we ask "according to his will" (1 John 5:14). Gifts are among the good things God gives (James 1:17), and it is God's will for us to have them and know them. If we ask in faith, God will not disappoint us.

17. What role does the family play in gift discovery and use?

First, parents are responsible to teach their children about spiritual things. In Deuteronomy 6:7 the Lord tells parents, "Impress [my commands] on your children. Talk about them when you sit at home and when you walk along the road, when you lie down and when you get up." In other words, parents are to teach their children about God in connection with all kinds of things they do in their everyday living. Parents are first in line when it comes to teaching children about gifts and ministries.

Second, parents are in the best position to observe each child's unique and developing abilities and to affirm each child as a gifted member of the body of Christ. God shapes the lives of his children for ministry from their earliest years. Alert parents can see and affirm spiritual gifts that God is developing in their children.

Third, Christian parents have an ongoing opportunity to set good examples for their children. Their modeling is particularly important in areas that will become a child's gift areas. For example, parents sharing their faith with others may lay important foundations for a child to whom God gives the gift of evangelism. Parents who give generously are models who establish patterns for their children who may also develop the gift of giving.

Finally, love must motivate the use of all gifts. Parents who, by their example, create a loving atmosphere in their home and a love for service in the kingdom of God prepare their children for love-motivated ministries in the future.

Section 4

18. How will the church benefit from understanding spiritual gifts?

The church is the body of Christ. Its members are mutually interdependent, caring for each other. Christ, its head, directs all the activities of the church. The life-giving Holy Spirit permeates all its parts. The body expresses the fullness of Christ, "who fills everything in every way" (Eph. 1:23).

The church needs spiritual gifts to reach its full potential as a life-sharing body. Since its life is expressed through gifted members ministering to one another, the absence of gifts and interdependent ministries signals the absence of body life. In *The Problem of Wineskins*, Howard Snyder underscores the need for understanding God's purpose for spiritual gifts in the church:

> The urgent need today is that spiritual gifts be seen and understood in the context of [the church], as in the New Testament. A biblical understanding of spiritual gifts is absolutely essential for a biblical conception of the church. . . . When spiritual gifts are misunderstood—through being individualized, denied, divorced from community, or otherwise distorted—it is the church which suffers. The church truly becomes the church only when the biblical meaning of spiritual gifts is recovered. A church whose life and ministry is not built upon the exercise of spiritual gifts is biblically a contradiction in terms.

The church will benefit from this, first, by awakening and mobilizing. Frozen assets will thaw. The church's unemployment problem will be solved. Stagnant congregations will come to life as each member begins to seek a rightful place in the community of Christ. The church will regain spiritual life and health.

Second, a heightened awareness of gifts will result in better leadership for the church. Pastors will be called and/or assigned on the basis of their gifts. Local congregations will be encouraged to choose officebearers on the basis of spiritual gifts. Leaders, functioning by the Spirit's power in the ministries for which they are gifted, will do their work well.

Third, a new spirit of unity will come to the church. In Ephesians 4 the apostle Paul declares that unity and Christlike maturity will result as equipped saints carry on the work of ministry. Members will feel more valuable and needed as they learn they are vital parts of the body of Christ. Members will develop a greater appreciation for one another as they recognize their mutual interdependence. Pursuit of programs, methods, and organizational objectives will become subservient to the pursuit of ministries flowing out of love.

Fourth, churches will be strengthened in evangelism as outreach-oriented gifts are developed. And if, in addition, gifts of hospitality and shepherding function well, new members will find their way into the body and the church will grow.

19. What happens when a church ignores spiritual gifts?

If a church does not help its members discover and use their spiritual gifts, it will suffer from the following problems:

- **An inactive, uninvolved membership.** An inactive church member is really a contradiction in terms. Membership in the true church equates with involvement in the ministries necessary to the life of the body. A church that is not gift-conscious is perpetuating the lie that one can truly be a member of the church of Christ by simply attending and "paying your dues."

- **An overworked minority.** The church that slights the teaching and development of spiritual gifts will have to rely on a minority to do its work. That minority, including the pastor, will be overworked, resulting in burnout and neglect of even the most essential tasks.

- **An unsatisfied communal life.** Without the communal use of gifts, there is no healthy communal life. Hurts are not healed. Needs are not met. Members do not talk about real problems and hurts or "carry each other's burdens" (Gal. 6:2), for few know the real burdens of others. Life in such a community may appear to be comfortable. But it is not a deeply caring, upbuilding community.

- **A lack of conversion growth.** A church indifferent to spiritual gifts will not need to worry about much conversion growth. Without the crucial gifts of evangelism, the church will win few converts. In addition, those who are converted through the church's ministries are not likely to stay in a church where the gift of hospitality is not operative. Further, new believers are not likely to grow if discipling gifts are not exercised.

- **Overdependence on programs.** If few members have ministries that flow from spiritual giftedness, the church will need to depend on programs to meet basic needs. But programs flop unless they are staffed by gifted, obedient people seeking to honor God in all they do.

20. What should we know about the misuse of spiritual gifts?

Almost every gift can be abused. Spiritual gifts are no exception. Spiritual gifts are sometimes misused in the church in the following ways:

- **Gift glorification.** In parts of the Christian community today the possession of certain spiritual gifts brings glory to a person. In some highly charismatic churches, for example, the manifestational gifts (such as miracles, healing, and tongues) are the most highly prized. People with these gifts are considered to be the most outstanding Christians. In institutional churches leadership gifts are often the most highly prized because of the prestige they carry. Glorifying certain gifts results in a hierarchy in which some gifted members become "special" while others, not possessing the same gifts, are seen as lesser or disregarded altogether. This leads to pride in some and inferiority feelings in others. Paul sternly warned the Corinthian church against exalting certain gifts (1 Cor. 12-14).

- **Gift projection.** Christians who think their particular gifts are the most important may project these gifts outward in such a way that others are made to feel ashamed and inferior if they don't have them. Peter Wagner calls this the "gift projection syndrome" (*Your Spiritual Gifts Can Help Your Church Grow*). This appears to have happened in Corinth (1 Cor. 12:14-26).

- **Gift denigration.** Overly confident, seemingly independent members of the body may fail to see how much they need to be ministered to by so-called weaker members. Paul counteracts the tendency to say "I don't need you" by reminding us that parts of the body that may seem weaker are actually "indispensable." Those whom we think are less honorable are worthy of "greater honor." God, he says, has made these variations in the body so that we may "have equal concern for each other." (See 1 Cor. 12:21-25.)

- **Gift individualization.** There is also a tendency to over-individualize spiritual gifts. Gifts are given to individuals, but they are given within the context of the Christian community. They are not meant for private use. They are given so that the body of Christ can be edified. In *The Problem of Wineskins*, Howard Snyder writes,

    The biblical conception is that the community of believers acts as the controlling context for the exercise of gifts, thus discouraging individualistic aberrations. And gifts must operate in this way. The church is, to use Gordon Cosby's phrase, "a gift-evoking, gift-bearing community." And when the church really functions in this way, the various gifts not only reinforce each other; they also act as checks and balances to prevent extremes.

Scripture emphasizes that gifts are "for the common good" (1 Cor. 12:7). They are to be used "so that the body of Christ may be built up until we all reach unity in the faith and in the knowledge of the Son of God and become mature, attaining to the whole measure of the fullness of Christ" (Eph. 4:12-13). Paul speaks not of a maturity in isolation but of a maturity in community.

21. How does gift-consciousness affect the church's structure?

The following changes can become a reality when a church begins to think seriously about spiritual gifts:

- **Selectivity in ministry assignments.** Most ministries in the church require selectivity. Not everyone should serve as a greeter, or go visiting door to door in the community, or hold an office in the church. The simple truth is that not everyone can do everything equally well. Thinking seriously about gifts will help the church avoid an "everyone-ought-to" mentality.

- **Opportunities for togetherness.** If gifts are to function well, the church needs to provide opportunities for members of the congregation to communicate freely with one another. Members cannot minister to one another or coordinate their efforts unless they get to know each other. Small groups, one of many structures that encourage informal and free exchange, help facilitate openness. Howard Snyder writes in *The Problem of Wineskins*, "Without the small group, the church in urban society simply does not experience one of the most basic essentials of the gospels—true, rich, deep Christian soul fellowship, or *koinonia*."

- **Ministry teams.** It is often helpful for a gifted person to develop a ministry with a group of people having related gifts and ministries. The church that provides ministry teams, task forces, or action groups actively encourages the use of gifts for ministry.

22. Do we have the potential to develop different gifts in the future?

It's important to know that while we have spiritual gifts that we are using right now, we often have the potential for developing various other gifts. As we grow more and more mature in Christ, God molds us and gifts us to serve in various ways—sometimes in ways we would not have pursued or even imagined without the guiding of the Holy Spirit.

Section 5

23. What are some intentional ways to develop my spiritual gifts?

- **Begin by studying Scripture.** Study passages that relate particularly to your gifts (see the Gift Studies section of this book). Study the lives of biblical characters who exercised gifts like yours. Study the roles related to your gifts.

- **Read books and articles** that expand your thinking in the area of your spiritual gifts. For example, resources such as *Now, Discover Your Strengths* and *Living Your Strengths* by Donald Clifton and others can help you find ways to put your spiritual gifts into practice. According to *Living Your Strengths*, knowing your spiritual gifts helps you find *what kinds* of ministries God wants you to be involved in; knowing your talents or strengths helps you see *how* you can be involved in those ministries. As the authors put it, "Identifying spiritual gifts defines the outcome; discovering talents defines the steps."

- **Talk to other Christians who have similar gifts.** They may be your best source of understanding your gifts. Learn what they have done with their gifts, what ministries they have developed, and what resources were most helpful to them.

- **Attend conferences, seminars, workshops, and classes** that will help you cultivate your gifts. Christians spend many hours in leisure-time classes and activities. Why not spend time in courses that aid gift development? If you can't get to a seminar because of distance or cost, it may be available on CD or DVD or the Internet. Don't be satisfied just to discover your gifts. Grow and mature in your gift abilities as you grow in spiritual maturity.

24. What can a spiritually gifted person do to find a ministry?

Don't wait to be asked to get involved in a ministry. Here are some specific ways to discover or develop a ministry:

- **Pray for guidance and strength.** Ask for strength to do what God calls you to do. Remember what Jesus says in John 15:5: "Apart from me you can do nothing." Ask God for guidance in knowing when, where, and how he wants to use your gifts. Ask the Father for the Holy Spirit (Luke 11:13). God is the source of all spiritual giftedness.

- **Be sensitive to the needs of others.** Pray for eyes to see needs that are both near and real. Look beneath the surface of people's lives to see hurts that cry out for healing. Try to meet some of the needs you discover. Spiritual gifts are the Holy Spirit's provisions for helping to meet human needs.

- **Focus your efforts in the area of your spiritual gifts.** Learn to say no to things that are not in line with your gifts. Get out of unfruitful activities. Establish priorities that will allow you time to develop a role in ministry. Then begin to use your gifts.

- **Be willing to begin small.** If, for example, you think you have the gift of evangelism, begin by seriously using it with just one other person. Or work alongside someone who is similarly gifted. If you have the gift of teaching, you may want to begin by sitting in on a church school class and observing the teacher.

- **Be yourself.** Remember that you are a unique person with an equally unique mix of gifts. Don't try to imitate anyone else. Your way of serving is probably God's best for you.

- **Be prepared to give yourself.** Jesus' threefold requirement for discipleship—"Deny yourself, take up your cross, and follow me" (see Matt. 16:24)—applies also to exercising your gifts. In *The Problem of Wineskins* Howard Snyder clearly focuses the issue of giving ourselves:

  > Ministry is not determined exclusively by personal desire, but by the cross. . . . As one is crucified with Christ and dies to his own will, the Holy Spirit resurrects within him his significant gift. So the spiritual gift, rightly exercised, is not self-centered; it is self-giving.

  > But we must go further than this. . . . Faithful ministry of the gift of the Spirit will lead . . . into depths of self-giving . . . never dreamed possible—and God planned it that way. This is the way we are created—psychologically, emotionally, and spiritually.

25. How can a church help its members develop spiritual gifts?
A church can do many things to help its people discover, develop, and use spiritual gifts for ministry:

- **Organize for ministry.** Take a fresh look at the structures of your church and ask, "Just how much real ministry is happening within the structures?" and, "How are the structures helping people to minister?" Leaders in the church need to see themselves as servants whose task is to help people develop ministries.

- **Recruit members on the basis of their gifts.** Unfortunately many church members serve where they do because they have not dared to say no or because they felt "somebody had to do it." A church can help its people develop gifts by assigning its gifted members to ministries that fit their gifts.

- **Equip for ministry.** "To equip [God's] people for works of service" (Eph. 4:12) is not simply a matter of theological training or on-the-job instruction. Rather, equipping should help people develop their spiritual gifts and the ministries related to them.

- **Provide support.** God does not intend for us to minister in isolation. Spiritually gifted members need to find personal support as they engage in ministry. By providing a healthy support structure, the church can facilitate gift ministries.

- **Be conscious of needs in the home, church, and community.** Since spiritual gifts are given to meet needs, the church that helps its members become more conscious of needs will also encourage the use of gifts. Awareness of needs may also lead to the development of new ministries designed to meet those needs.

- **Affirm spiritual gifts.** All gifts and gifted members are important. Church leaders who affirm this in words and actions will help members develop self-esteem and confidence in service.

26. How do spiritual gifts help Christians minister outside the church?

The ministries of the church extend not only to those on the membership rolls but also to people and institutions outside the church. The presence of Christ is not limited to the sanctuary; nor are the gifts he has given to his people. The church must live out its life in the world, use its spiritual gifts, and make an impact for Christ.

People, groups, and institutions in the world are all objects of God's concern. The world too is called to give account to Jesus Christ as Lord. It needs to hear the good news of God's salvation and to be reshaped by the Holy Spirit's transforming power. As the body of Christ in the world, the church is the bearer of this good news. The church itself is evidence that Christ cares for the world, and in the midst of the world the church is to be a spiritually gifted, loving, and ministering organism.

27. How do spiritual gifts relate to ministry passions?

A passion is something that you deeply care about, something that drives you. Spiritual gifts often combine naturally with a passion that serves to motivate. For example, a person with the gift of evangelism will usually be passionately concerned for the salvation of others. A person with the gift of mercy will passionately care about people who are hurting.

But it is also possible for a person to have passions that lie outside his or her main gift area. If that is the case, those passions may help determine a context or method for using one's gifts effectively. For example, a person with gifts of organization and leadership and a passion for evangelism will want to use those gifts to lead and organize evangelistic ministries. A similarly gifted person with a passion for helping people in great need may want to use his or her gifts to organize a program to help such hurting persons.

Our passions guide us in choosing where to focus our gifts. If you are passionate about a particular cause such as abortion, addictions, marriage and family, HIV/AIDS, poverty, environmental care, pornography, or physical fitness, you could use any of a number of gifts to minister in that area. It would not be hard to imagine using your gift of leadership, organization, intercession, giving, encouragement, service, or teaching in any of these areas.

To find clues to your ministry passion, you need to think about things and activities that excite you. What areas most interest you? What do you think is an important problem that needs to be addressed?

GIFT STUDIES

ADMINISTRATION

Definition

The Spirit-given ability to design and execute a plan of action through which a number of believers are enabled to work effectively together to do the Lord's work.

Administration as a Spiritual Gift

The gift of administration is identified in 1 Corinthians 12:28 (NIV, RSV, NKJV). Some Bible versions translate the Greek word here as "guidance" (TNIV); others as "leadership" (NRSV, CEV); and others in terms of directing (TEV) and governing (NCV, KJV, ASV). The Greek word for administration—*kubernasis*—means "one who guides or directs toward a goal." It was commonly used to identify one who steers or pilots a ship. An able pilot had the ability to keep the ship and crew sailing smoothly to the next port. The word was also used to describe the manager of a household. As a spiritual gift, administration has to do with a God-given ability to guide the affairs of the kingdom of God. The person with this gift brings organizational and management skills to the body of Christ.

This gift has also been called the gift of organization. But this does not necessarily mean the administrator has a neat desk and well-organized files. In the church this person gives clear guidance to the process of ministry and facilitates the activities of people working together toward kingdom goals. The gifted administrator is able to get things done through people by directing, motivating, and coordinating their activities. Nehemiah, for example, was an expert administrator, motivating and harmonizing the activities of many hundreds of people as they rebuilt the walls of Jerusalem (Neh. 2-7).

The gift of administration mentioned in 1 Corinthians 12:28 should be distinguished from the gift of leadership (Rom. 12:8). The two are related but different. The leader envisions the future and sets goals; the administrator devises the plans to accomplish the goals. The leader knows where the port is; the administrator knows how to navigate the ship into the port. The leader holds out the vision for ministry; the administrator helps to translate the vision into reality by developing a plan of action and directing other believers in the process. While the gifts of administration and leadership are different, it is not uncommon for one person to have both.

The gift of administration can be used in many different ways. A person with this gift will usually take an organized approach to daily activities such as personal devotions, time management, and family life. In the life of the church he or she will be a model committee member, coordinator, director, superintendent, or planner. On a board this person will provide valuable insights into managing a system and achieving goals.

Characteristics of the Spiritually Gifted Administrator
- able to organize ideas, tasks, people, and time to achieve an objective
- able to make effective plans to achieve goals
- able to delegate important tasks to the right people at the right time

Some Ways to Use the Gift of Administration
Personal/informal uses:

- organize family devotions
- help a friend develop a family budget
- organize a neighborhood get-together

Ministries within the church:

- oversee education programs
- direct a program
- chair a committee

Community-oriented ministries for Christ:

- organize a fund-raising campaign
- serve on the board of a home for elderly people
- organize a rally

Potential Liabilities in the Gift of Administration
The spiritually gifted administrator can sometimes tend to

- rely on well-organized plans rather than on the power of the Spirit and on direction from God through prayer.
- think of projects as more important than the people who are needed to get the projects done.
- "take over" in such a way as to leave little room for other people's ideas and concerns.
- be too careful and block progress toward an overall vision.

Administration as a Responsibility of All Christians
An administrator devises effective plans and carries them out to accomplish a task. All people are administrators in their own lives. Jesus calls us to plan wisely and effectively. He expects believers to live wisely and plan well by building on a solid foundation (Matt. 7:24-27; Luke 14:28-30). Scripture warns against planning that leaves out the Lord (James 4:13-15).

Exploring Administration from Scripture

1. Write out the part of 1 Corinthians 12:28 that refers to this gift.

2. How does Jethro exercise the gift of administration in Exodus 18:12-27?

3. How does Nehemiah exercise this gift? (See Neh. 4:11-23.)

4. How did the appointment of deacons with administrative gifts help the newly founded Jerusalem church (Acts 6:1-7)?

CREATIVE ABILITY

Definition

The Spirit-given ability to communicate truth and advance God's kingdom creatively through music, drama, visual arts, and/or writing skills.

Creative Ability as a Spiritual Gift

Some Christians have distinctive creative abilities they are called to use in the service of the King. For example, Bezalel and Oholiab, associates of Moses, were given unique abilities by the Holy Spirit. As Exodus 35:30-35 tells us,

> Moses said to the Israelites, "See, the LORD has chosen Bezalel son of Uri, the son of Hur, of the tribe of Judah, and he has filled him with the Spirit of God, with wisdom, with understanding, with knowledge and with all kinds of skills—to make artistic designs for work in gold, silver and bronze, to cut and set stones, to work in wood and to engage in all kinds of artistic crafts. And he has given both him and Oholiab son of Ahisamak, of the tribe of Dan, the ability to teach others. He has filled them with skill to do all kinds of work as engravers, designers, embroiderers in blue, purple and scarlet yarn and fine linen, and weavers—all of them skilled workers and designers."

God gave these gifts in order to build and beautify the tabernacle and thus to promote centralized worship for the people of God as they traveled to the promised land of Canaan.

Music is a creative ability mentioned in Scripture. David was uniquely gifted as a musician and songwriter (2 Sam. 23:1). His great poetic ability was a skill God used to enhance temple worship. David's psalms have blessed the church throughout the ages. Musicians also were specially appointed because of their creative abilities (1 Chron. 16:41-42; 2 Chron. 5:12-13).

Gift Studies

Characteristics of the Person with Creative Ability

- use of a particular creative talent (such as writing, painting, drama, music, graphic arts, sculpting) to benefit the body of Christ
- able to communicate divine truth visually, graphically, or vocally in interesting, imaginative, and inspiring ways
- through this person's artistic efforts, people are spiritually stimulated and grow in their appreciation of God and his world

Some Ways to Use the Gift of Creative Ability

Personal/informal uses:

- make music or other art for personal enjoyment
- keep a daily journal or write a family history or insightful articles
- assist a friend in home decoration

Ministries within the church:

- sing in a church group
- write music, poetry, litanies, or prayers for use in worship
- design liturgical banners
- lead the craft time in a children's class
- participate in a worship drama or liturgical dance

Community-oriented ministries for Christ:

- do freelance writing
- assist in a community arts festival
- act in a dramatic presentation of the life of Christ

Potential Liabilities in the Gift of Creative Ability

A person with this gift can sometimes tend to

- assume the ability is a natural talent and not be concerned to use it for Christ and his kingdom.
- use the ability for self-glory.
- fail to develop the gift because of laziness.
- look down on persons with other gifts.

Creative Ability as a Responsibility of All Christians

All Christians are called to exercise creative imagination in their daily activities. While God gave special abilities to Bezalel and Oholiab, he also gave skill to all the artisans and designers building the temple (Ex. 31:6; 36:2). Often it's in worship that we have opportunity to give expression to creative abilities. Paul, for example, encourages all believers to speak "to one another with psalms, hymns, and songs from the Spirit. Sing and make music from your heart to the Lord" (Eph. 5:19; see also Col. 3:16-17).

Exploring Creative Ability from Scripture

1. Read Exodus 31:1-6 and 35:30-35. What distinctive creative abilities did God give to Bezalel and Oholiab and others?

2. What, in addition to skill, was required of a person involved in the work of building the place of worship? (See Ex. 36:2.)

4. What place did music and dance have in temple worship? (See Ps. 149:1-4; 150.)

5. Why were special musical gifts given, according to 1 Chronicles 25:6-7?

DISCERNMENT

Definition

The Spirit-given ability to know whether a statement, action, or motive has its source in God, our sinful human nature, or Satan.

Discernment as a Spiritual Gift

Paul speaks of discernment as a spiritual gift, calling it the ability of "distinguishing between spirits" (1 Cor. 12:10). This phrase suggests a supernatural ability to detect the difference between a message from the Holy Spirit and a message from evil spirits who pretend to speak for God.

Jesus regularly used this gift. When Peter opposed his going to Jerusalem to suffer, Jesus discerned the source behind his comment and responded, "Get behind me, Satan!" (Matt. 16:23). When Jewish teachers of the law said of Jesus, "This fellow is blaspheming!" Jesus, knowing their thoughts, asked, "Why do you entertain evil thoughts in your hearts?" (Matt. 9:3-4).

The apostles also used the gift of discernment. When Ananias and Sapphira tested the early Christian community with their lies, Peter discerned their deceit and pronounced judgment upon them (Acts 5:1-11). When Simon the sorcerer sought the gift of the Holy Spirit with wrong motives, Peter urged him to repent, seeing that he was "full of bitterness and captive to sin" (Acts 8:9-25). Paul, "filled with the Holy Spirit," discerned the true source of Elymas's opposition to the gospel and said, "You are a child of the devil and an enemy of everything that is right! You are full of all kinds of deceit and trickery" (Acts 13:9-10). Paul also detected and cast out an evil spirit that had possessed a slave girl, whose owners were using her to tell fortunes (Acts 16:16-18).

There is both a natural and a supernatural dimension to discerning. Persons who have this gift will naturally be able to spot motives and attitudes, sniff out hypocrites, and distinguish truth from error, even if these are not directly associated with evil spirits. Many theologians and faithful biblical scholars possess this gift and use it to help protect the church from heresy. But sometimes the gift operates supernaturally as the Holy Spirit gives the discerner, through an inner knowing, awareness of demonic or subversive influence in the words, actions, or motives of another person. Discernment often functions together with the gifts of wisdom and knowledge.

The church has always needed this gift. There were many false teachers and prophets seeking to deceive believers (Matt. 7:15; Mark 13:22). Peter says, "They will secretly introduce destructive heresies," and "many will follow . . . and will bring the way of truth into dispute" (2 Pet. 2:1-2). Paul warned about "deceiving spirits and things taught by demons" (1 Tim. 4:1) and of rulers, authorities, powers of darkness, and spiritual forces of evil that we must struggle against (Eph. 6:12). Satan, "the father of lies," is ever seeking to pervert the truth (John 8:44).

The gift of discernment is given by the Spirit to help protect the church from taking wrong pathways. Although all believers are to test prophecies (1 Thess. 5:21) and "test the spirits to see whether they are from God" (1 John 4:1), members who have the gift of discernment have a heightened ability and responsibility to do so. Discernment should be tested in community with others, especially in matters of great importance for the church.

Characteristics of the Person with the Gift of Discernment
- able to detect phony persons and false teachings
- able to perceive people's true spiritual motivation
- able to tell when a person is controlled or influenced by an evil spirit

Some Ways to Use the Gift of Discernment
Personal/informal uses:

- warn people about false teachings
- stand against persons who have wrong motives or deceitful purposes
- protect people from the dangers of false teaching in the church and society

Ministries within the church:

- help with interviewing people for ministry positions
- evaluate study materials
- engage in spiritual warfare through prayer

Community-oriented ministries for Christ:

- counsel people who have been taken in by satanic influences
- identify and work against evil and destructive forces in societal structures (for example, racism, oppression of the poor, corruption in government or in the court system)

Potential Liabilities in the Gift of Discernment

A person with this gift can sometimes tend to

- become an overzealous heresy hunter.
- be tempted to have a proud, critical, or judgmental spirit.
- unnecessarily attack and berate people.
- withdraw from the church because it is less than perfect.

Discernment as a Responsibility of All Christians

Many voices clamor to be heard today. Every Christian needs to be discerning. The Holy Spirit gives every believer the capacity to discern good from evil in order to live a life of godliness (Phil. 1:9-11). The psalmist pleads, "I am your servant; give me discernment that I may understand your statutes" (Ps. 119:125). Hebrews 5:14 speaks of this gift as the mark of a mature Christian. John encourages all believers to distinguish between truth and error (1 John 4:1). Paul writes that any person who has the Holy Spirit can test the validity of spiritual teachings (1 Cor. 2:14-15). Full of the Holy Spirit, believers will increasingly be able to see as Christ sees.

Exploring Discernment from Scripture

1. How does Satan try to corrupt the church? (See 2 Cor. 11:13-15; Eph. 6:11-12.)

2. According to 2 Peter 2:1-3, how do false teachers work? What effect do they have on the church?

3. How is the church to deal with false spirits and teachers? What is the test by which they are measured? How is the spirit of truth known? (See 1 John 4:1-3, 6.)

4. How was the gift of discernment used in each of the following situations? What were the results?

    - Matthew 16:21-23
    - Acts 5:1-11
    - Acts 13:6-12

ENCOURAGEMENT

Definition

The Spirit-given ability to effectively encourage, comfort, challenge, or rebuke others to help them live lives worthy of God.

Encouragement as a Spiritual Gift

Encouragement is identified as a spiritual gift in Romans 12:8. The emphasis of the Greek word *parakaleo* in that passage is fundamentally positive. Even when the connotation is "to rebuke," it means doing so in order to bring about positive change. This Greek term denotes standing alongside another person to encourage, support, or console as well as to challenge, urge, or rebuke, where necessary, for spiritual growth and to "spur one another on toward love and good deeds" (Heb. 10:24). This gift is sometimes described as the gift of counseling.

Many people in the New Testament exercised this gift. Paul and Barnabas strengthened and encouraged "a large number of disciples" to "remain true to the faith" (Acts 14:21-22). In fact, Barnabas, whose name means "son of encouragement," encouraged and discipled both Paul (Saul) and Mark (Acts 4:36; 9:26-28; 11:25-26; 12:25). Peter encouraged the elders of the churches in Asia Minor to be diligent and faithful in their work (1 Pet. 5:1-3).

The role of the gifted encourager is similar to that of the Holy Spirit, who is also called the "Counselor" or "Comforter." These names derive from the same root as the word for encouragement (see John 14:16, 26). The Holy Spirit stands alongside a believer in order to help. So too the spiritually gifted encourager, enabled by the Spirit, becomes a channel for the comfort and counsel of the divine Encourager.

Characteristics of the Person with the Gift of Encouragement

- spurs people on "to love and good deeds" by means of counsel and encouragement, guided by the Holy Spirit
- sees the potential in people and urges them to serve God to the best of their ability
- regularly ministers to others by offering practical counsel and guidance for spiritual growth

Some Ways to Use the Gift of Encouragement

Personal/informal uses:

- counsel a friend with a problem
- encourage a new Christian
- serve as a spiritual mentor or "soulmate"

Gift Studies

Ministries within the church:

- visit and counsel inactive members
- serve as an inspirational speaker
- help others find ways to use their gifts in ministry

Community-oriented ministries for Christ:

- serve at an ex-offender contact center
- be a mentor for neighborhood teens
- counsel at a crisis-pregnancy center

Potential Liabilities in the Gift of Encouragement

A person with this gift can sometimes tend to

- create dependencies by getting too involved in people's lives.
- overextend in counseling people and neglect other important duties.
- be satisfied with easy solutions to complex problems.

Encouragement as a Responsibility of All Christians

All Christians are called to care for and encourage one another. Hebrews 3:13 says, "Encourage one another daily." Paul challenges believers to "encourage one another and build each other up" (1 Thess. 5:11). The same kind of responsibility is laid on Christians in Hebrews 10:24-25: "Let us consider how we may spur one another on toward love and good deeds . . . encouraging one another."

Exploring Encouragement from Scripture

1. What did Paul do with this gift, according to Acts 20:28-31 and 1 Thessalonians 5:14-22?

2. What should be the attitude of one who encourages, according to 1 Thessalonians 2:11-12?

3. What evidence does the Bible give that Barnabas had the gift of encouragement? (See Acts 4:36; 9:26-28; 11:25-26; 12:25.)

4. How does the role of the gifted encourager compare to that of the Holy Spirit?

EVANGELISM

Definition

The Spirit-given ability to present the gospel to unbelievers in clear and meaningful ways that bring a positive response.

Evangelism as a Spiritual Gift

Ephesians 4:11 identifies the gift of evangelism by pointing to persons who have this gift—evangelists. The New Testament signals the operation of this gift in many situations. Philip was a gifted and effective evangelist (Acts 8:4-40; 21:8). Paul and Barnabas "won a large number of disciples" by exercising their gift of evangelism as they preached the good news in Asia Minor (Acts 14:21). In 2 Timothy 4:5 Paul encourages Timothy the pastor to "do the work of an evangelist."

The objective of the gift of evangelism is to bring unbelievers to faith in Jesus Christ and into the church. This gift, used both in one-to-one situations and in public settings, is also useful in the structure of the local church. The evangelist works with other leaders in the church "to prepare God's people for works of service" (Eph. 4:11-12). This will happen as the evangelistically gifted person serves as an example and trains those who may have yet to discover and develop this spiritual gift. In addition, leaders who have the gift will lift up the vision and practice of outreach. Administrators who have the gift will help to organize evangelistic ministries. Teachers who have the gift will instruct others in evangelism methods. According to Peter Wagner in *Your Spiritual Gifts Can Help Your Church Grow*, 5 to 10 percent of the adult members of a local church are likely to have the gift of evangelism.

Characteristics of the Spiritually Gifted Evangelist

- able, in the Spirit's power, to clearly present the message of salvation to unbelievers
- lead others, with the Spirit's help, to believe in Christ as Savior

Some Ways to Use the Gift of Evangelism

Personal/informal uses:

- witness to those who do not know Jesus
- lead family members to commitment to Christ

Ministries within the church:

- participate in outreach efforts
- lead an evangelistic Bible study
- share the gospel with children and/or adults in a Bible school setting

Community-oriented ministries for Christ:

- become involved in a marketplace ministry
- give an evangelistic message at a rescue mission
- counsel at an evangelistic crusade

Potential Liabilities in the Gift of Evangelism

The spiritually gifted evangelist can sometimes tend to

- rely on his or her own power of expression or persuasion to convert people.
- take pride in the number of converts won.
- pass negative judgment on others who don't have the gift.

Evangelism as a Responsibility of All Christians

To evangelize is to bring the good news of Christ's salvation to unbelievers. Not all Christians are evangelists, but all believers are called to share the good news of Jesus (evangelize). All Christians whose hearts are in tune with God will want "all people to be saved and to come to a knowledge of the truth" (1 Tim. 2:4). All Christians share responsibility to carry out the Lord's great commission (Matt. 28:18-20). All are involved in bringing the good news "to the ends of the earth" (Acts 1:8). All are also called to spread the Word of God whenever and wherever there is opportunity (Acts 8:4).

Exploring Evangelism from Scripture

1. Write out the portions of Ephesians 4:11-12 and 2 Timothy 4:5 that identify evangelism as a gift.

2. What does Philip's example tell us about the work of an evangelist, as described in Acts 8:5-6, 12, 26-40?

3. Read Mark 1:16-17. In this passage, to whom was the gift of evangelism given?

4. What does Jesus teach his disciples about the power of the Holy Spirit and the gift of evangelism in Acts 1:8?

FAITH

Definition

The Spirit-given ability to know that God wills to do something, even when there is no concrete evidence to support that conviction.

Faith as a Spiritual Gift

The person with the spiritual gift of faith has a special ability to trust that God can and will work with amazing power in specific situations. This Spirit-given ability connects closely with knowing what God wants to do in this world and how God wants to accomplish it. The confidence of the gift of faith comes from an inner conviction supplied by the Holy Spirit. It is not a contrived mental attitude dependent on the strength of one's own belief.

The spiritual gift of faith (1 Cor. 12:9) should be distinguished from saving faith, the faith on which our redemption rests. Saving faith is the God-given ability to trust in the atoning work of Christ for our salvation.

Though not much is said in Scripture about the spiritual gift of faith, there are many evidences of its use. Abraham used this gift when he obeyed God's call on various occasions and when he responded to Isaac's question about a lamb for sacrifice, saying, "God himself will provide the lamb" (Gen. 22:8; see Heb. 11:8-19). Jesus used this gift when he said with absolute confidence to the sister of Lazarus, who had died, "Your brother will rise again" (John 11:23). Peter acted with the gift of faith when he stepped out of a boat and walked on water at Jesus' invitation (Matt. 14:28-29). Paul exercised this gift in a dangerous situation when he trusted God's word that he would not be harmed, and he continued to preach with boldness (Acts 18:9-11). God also gave Paul the faith to know that he and everyone with him would be spared from drowning, even though the ship they were sailing on would be wrecked (Acts 27:21-26).

God uses the gift of faith in many ways. God brings glory to himself as believers who have this gift honor God's name in the face of adversity. The church is encouraged to remember that God is in control of all things. The gift of faith helps individuals and churches to face crises with confidence and to meet challenges with boldness. Jesus was likely referring to this gift when he spoke of faith that could move mountains (Matt. 21:21-22; see 1 Cor. 13:2).

Characteristics of the Person with the Gift of Faith

- know with certainty that God has willed to do something
- able to trust God to intervene in supernatural ways in spite of evidence to the contrary

Some Ways to Use the Gift of Faith

Personal/informal uses:

- firmly trust God's promise for a family member or friend
- may be used to bring healing through "the prayer of faith" (see James 5:13-18)

Ministries within the church:

- challenge and/or lead the church to renewal
- help keep up hope in a discouraging situation

Community-oriented ministry for Christ:

- know and trust God's will toward developing a new ministry

Potential Liabilities in the Gift of Faith

A person with the gift of faith can sometimes tend to

- pass judgment on those who do not have such faith.
- exercise the gift of faith without love (1 Cor. 13:2).
- be impatient with others who are cautious or uncertain.

Faith as a Responsibility of All Christians

Some Christians have the spiritual gift of faith, but every Christian must have saving faith to be a Christian. Jesus encourages all to believe (John 6:29; 14:1) and makes faith the ground of salvation (John 20:31). Believers are saved by grace through faith (Eph. 2:8). In addition, all believers are called to trust God in all circumstances of life, believing that the Lord will keep his promises and work things out "for the good of those who love him" (Rom. 8:28). Those who trust God fully are blessed and rewarded (Heb. 11:39-40).

Exploring Faith from Scripture

1. What is the difference between the gift of faith identified in 1 Corinthians 12:9 and the saving faith mentioned in Romans 3:22 and 5:1-2?

2. Read Romans 4:18-22 and Hebrews 11:11-12. Who exercised this gift? What was the ground of his confidence? The result?

3. What motive is essential when exercising the gift of faith (see 1 Cor. 13:2)? What is likely to happen if this motive is absent?

4. What is the value of the gift of faith in the Christian life (Heb. 11:32-40)? How do you explain the fact that some of these heroes of faith seemed to go down to defeat (11:35-40)?

GIVING

Definition

The Spirit-given ability to contribute significant personal and material resources to the Lord's work freely, cheerfully, and sacrificially.

Giving as a Spiritual Gift

The spiritual gift of giving is identified in Romans 12:8 along with several other gifts. The Greek word used to describe this gift implies a sense of giving or sharing of ourselves as we give. This involves giving that responds to a specific need, giving in which we share not only our resources but also ourselves. The gift of giving celebrates the compassionate concern of the giver.

The gift of giving does not belong only to high-income people. For example, Paul's Christian friends in Macedonia were poor, but by the grace of God "their extreme poverty welled up in rich generosity" so that they gave "even beyond their ability" (2 Cor. 8:1-3). The amount that is given is less important than the attitude and spirit of the giver.

Jesus commended the spirit of self-sacrifice as a model for all of us when he saw a poor widow give all that she had (Luke 21:1-3). Dorcas too was a fine example of a person with a giving attitude: she gave of her own material goods, and she gave freely of her spiritual gifts (creative ability, mercy, service) to help clothe the poor (Acts 9:36-39). In bringing the gospel, the apostles (and their many companions) also gave freely of their entire lives—many of them were even executed for their faith.

While some individuals have the spiritual gift of giving, all believers have the responsibility to give. How do these differ? The spiritually gifted giver is distinguished by a willing attitude and spirit. The apostle Paul's attitude toward the Thessalonian Christians illustrates this. He said to them, "Because we loved you so much, we were delighted to share with you not only the gospel of God but our lives as well" (1 Thess. 2:8). This passage uses the same Greek word that Romans 12:8 uses to identify the gift of giving. Gifted givers have a strong interest in the people and the causes they support; they see money and all their resources as a way to serve God.

Characteristics of the Spiritually Gifted Giver

- finds great joy in giving, looking for ways to meet people's needs by giving of oneself as well as one's material resources
- gives freely and cheerfully, often above what is expected
- takes a strong personal interest in causes and people who need support, and sees giving as a way to minister

Some Ways to Use the Gift of Giving

Personal/informal uses:

- assist a person financially
- help a Christian friend discover the joy of giving
- make a strategic, no-interest loan
- practice giving of time and talents to serve others

Ministries within the church:

- contribute generously from material goods and one's area of giftedness
- teach a stewardship class
- give liberally to kingdom causes

Community-oriented ministries for Christ:

- support a charity organization with regular gifts
- invest "seed money" in a worthy cause
- assist in organizing a fund drive

Potential Liabilities in the Gift of Giving

People with this gift can sometimes tend to

- be proud of their generosity.
- condemn as unspiritual those who do not give self-sacrificially.
- try to buy influence or position with their gifts.
- be unduly critical of how others spend money.

Giving as a Responsibility of All Christians

Even if only some believers have the spiritual gift of giving, all believers are challenged to give. Scripture teaches, "Each of you must bring a gift in proportion to the way the LORD your God has blessed you" (Deut. 16:17). And "if the willingness is there, the gift is acceptable according to what one has, not according to what one does not have" (2 Cor. 8:12). Further, Proverbs 3:9-10 says, "Honor the LORD with your wealth, with the firstfruits of all your crops; then your barns will be filled to overflowing, and your vats will brim over with new wine." When we give freely of all we have to the Lord, trusting that he will provide all we need, God graciously gives more than we need so that we can keep on giving—for the upbuilding and strengthening of the kingdom (2 Cor. 9:8-11).

Exploring Giving from Scripture

1. Acts 4:32-37 shows how the gift of giving functioned in the early church. What were the results of this giving in the Christian community?

2. What do we learn about the function of giving in Luke 8:1-3?

3. What can we learn from 2 Corinthians 8:1-7 about exercising the gift of giving?

4. According to 2 Corinthians 9:6-15, how are we to give? How are we able to give? What promise does God make to the giver? What's the result in the Christian community?

HEALING

Definition

The Spirit-given ability to serve as an instrument through whom God brings physical, emotional, and spiritual healing in both ordinary and extraordinary ways.

Healing as a Spiritual Gift

Healing is identified as a spiritual gift in 1 Corinthians 12:9: "To another [is given] gifts of healing by that one Spirit." Note that "gifts" here is plural, suggesting a variety of abilities relating to physical, emotional, and spiritual healing.

Jesus often exercised gifts of healing. The Bible reports thirty-eight times that Jesus was involved in individual or multiple healings. In addition, the book of Acts identifies seventeen healings by the Lord's apostles. James assigns to elders the task of praying for the sick. They are to offer prayers "in faith [that] will make [sick persons] well; the Lord will raise them up" (James 5:15). There is no indication that Jesus expected healing ministries of this type to discontinue before his return.

The purpose of healing gifts, as well as other spiritual gifts, is to testify to the gospel (Heb. 2:4). Through gifts of healing, God shows his concern for our physicial bodies as well as our souls. The ultimate goal of the kingdom of God is wholeness in Christ.

Gifts of healing do not do away with the need for doctors and nurses. In fact, many medical people may have this gift. God is glorified through healing by medical means as well as by extraordinary means. There are no universally valid means of healing given in Scripture. Faith, prayer, anointing, a word of command, and laying on of hands are often but not always mentioned. Oil, ointments, herbs, and spices are also mentioned as accompanying healing. There is no "magic formula" in healing. People with potential for gifts of healing also have unusual compassion for the sick. Further, guidance by the Spirit in healing is essential. The gifts of healing may be linked to the gift of faith in such a way that the individual knows that God will heal in a specific situation.

Characteristics of the Person with the Gift of Healing

- faith that God can and does heal in both natural and supernatural ways
- able to pray expectantly for persons who are physically, emotionally, or spiritually ill
- able to minister to people in a way that brings God's healing

Some Ways to Use the Gift of Healing

Personal/informal uses:

- pray in faith with persons who are sick, lay on hands, and anoint with oil as led by the Spirit
- respond to prayer concerns through the power of the Spirit to help sick and suffering persons

Ministries within the church:

- join an intercession team
- get involved in ministries to hurting people
- accompany pastors or church shepherds as they make pastoral visits
- be a designated intercessor in a need-based support group

Community-oriented ministries for Christ:

- work alongside doctors by praying for the well-being of persons who need healing
- serve as a volunteer at a medical or psychiatric hospital
- become involved with a national cancer society, AIDS organization, or other agency offering care services to the community

Potential Liabilities in the Gift of Healing

A person with this gift can sometimes tend to

- try to heal anyone at any time, without appropriate discernment of the Spirit's guidance.
- become unyielding about using methods not confirmed in Scripture.
- make healing dependent on a sick person's faith.
- take credit for healing instead of giving glory to God.
- become impatient when healing doesn't happen.
- place more emphasis on healing by supernatural means than by natural means.

Healing as a Responsibility of All Christians

God can use every Christian to bring healing. Sometimes God works through healing teams. Emotional healing may come through believers who are able to listen in a loving and sympathetic way. Spiritual healing may happen through believers who exhort and encourage. Because the healing Spirit resides in all believers, God can use us all.

Exploring Healing from Scripture

1. What do Exodus 15:26; 23:25; and Psalm 103:3 teach us about God and healing?

2. Read Matthew 9:35 and Mark 6:56. How integral would you say healing was to Jesus' ministry? What do Acts 10:38 and 1 John 3:8 teach us about Jesus' healing ministry? What is the purpose of healing, according to Hebrews 2:4?

3. Who was responsible for Paul's affliction described in 2 Corinthians 12:7-10? Why did God not heal him and remove the affliction? What does this teach us about God's readiness to heal? Should any person with enough faith expect to be healed?

4. What does 2 Kings 20:1-7 show us about God's use of ordinary and extraordinary means to heal?

HOSPITALITY

Definition

The Spirit-given ability to welcome and graciously serve guests and strangers so that they feel at home.

Hospitality as a Spiritual Gift

The apostle Peter mentions hospitality in a way that shows it's a gift of the Holy Spirit, conferred on the church for building up the body and for community ministry (1 Pet. 4:8-10). The word *hospitable* literally means "given to love of strangers." The hospitable person is one who is comfortable entertaining not only friends or relatives but also strangers. Hospitable people are able to make others feel at ease and cared for in their presence, in their home, or in their church. The comfort of the guest or stranger is a priority higher than the gifted person's own comfort. Believers who have this gift truly love hosting others.

God himself demonstrated hospitality by loving strangers from all nations: "These [strangers] I will bring to my holy mountain and give them joy in my house of prayer" (Isa. 56:7). Jesus exercised this gift when he welcomed sinners and ate with them (Luke 15:1-2), and he challenged his followers to "invite the poor, the crippled, the lame, [and] the blind" instead of focusing only on friends and relatives (Luke 14:12-14). Lydia exemplified this gift by showing hospitality to Paul and his companions (Acts 16:14-15).

Readiness to provide food and lodging was particularly important in the first century, which lacked a system of guest facilities for everyday travelers. Diotrephes was reprimanded for failing to show hospitality (3 John 9-10). Gaius was commended for his hospitality to strangers (3 John 5-8).

Characteristics of the Person with the Gift of Hospitality

- enjoy providing a haven for guests without feeling imposed upon
- able to help strangers feel at ease in one's home and at church
- always willing to open one's home and heart to people in need of hospitality

Some Ways to Use the Gift of Hospitality

Personal/informal uses:

- display gracious openness to strangers
- entertain in one's home
- welcome travelers and others who are temporarily away from home

Ministries within the church:

- be a greeter or usher
- make welcome visits to people who have moved into the church neighborhood
- help new members get assimilated
- host the church's coffee hour

Community-oriented ministries for Christ:

- be a receptionist at a nursing home
- befriend foreign students
- get involved in refugee or ex-offender resettlement

Potential Liabilities in the Gift of Hospitality

A person with this gift can sometimes tend to

- allow people to take undue advantage of his or her hospitality.
- come on too strong and overwhelm reticent people.
- not be able to say no when he or she really should.

Hospitality as a Responsibility of All Christians

The Bible encourages all Christians to be hospitable. God told his people in the Old Testament, "When foreigners reside among you in your land . . . [treat them] as your native-born. Love them as yourself, for you were foreigners in Egypt" (Lev. 19:33-34). Paul includes the command "practice hospitality" in his list of Christian responsibilities in Romans 12:9-21. And Hebrews 13:2 states, "Do not forget to show hospitality to strangers."

Exploring Hospitality from Scripture

1. With what attitude should hospitality be offered, according to 1 Peter 4:8-9?

2. Read Acts 16:14-15. How did Lydia exemplify the gift of hospitality?

3. What did Jesus teach and show in connection with hospitality? (See Matt. 25:34-40; Luke 14:12-14; 15:1-2.)

INTERCESSION

Definition

The Spirit-given ability to pray faithfully and effectively for others for extended periods and to see many specific answers to those prayers.

Intercession as a Spiritual Gift

Scripture includes many examples of extraordinary ministries of intercession. Our Lord's example in prayer stands out above all. The gospels record eighteen references to Jesus' prayer life, eight prayers that he prayed, and fourteen different prayer themes about which he taught. Two passages also speak of Jesus' ongoing high-priestly ministry of prayer from heaven (Rom. 8:34; Heb. 7:25).

Paul's record of interceding on behalf of the churches he established is also remarkable. On ten occasions in his letters to churches, Paul describes his intercessory prayers for them (see, for example, 1 Thess. 1:2-3).

In the Old Testament Abraham stands out as an intercessor in his earnest prayer for people in Sodom (Gen. 18:22-33). Moses interceded faithfully and effectively for disobedient Israel (Ex. 32:31-32; Ps. 106:23). Samuel too interceded faithfully for God's people, saying, "Far be it from me that I should sin against the LORD by failing to pray for you" (1 Sam. 12:23). Elijah was also an example of a righteous person whose prayers were "powerful and effective" (James 5:16-18; see 1 Kings 17:21-22; 18:42-45).

The Old Testament (Hebrew) word for this kind of prayer means "to assail God with requests." The New Testament (Greek) word for "intercession" conveys the idea of "a heartfelt concern for others in which one stands between them and God making request on their behalf" (*Baker Dictionary of Theology*). Intercession is, however, more than verbal requests. It involves a way of life, for one cannot intercede without a willingness to be involved. The one who stands between God and someone else represents both; pleading the person's cause to God and representing God's concern to the person.

Characteristics of the Spiritually Gifted Intercessor

- considers the prayer requests of others seriously, and prays for them for extended periods
- agonizes over and identifies with the people being prayer for
- conscious of ministering to others while praying for them, releasing God's power and grace in their lives

Some Ways to Use the Gift of Intercession

Personal/informal uses:

- faithfully intercede for friends, family, and others
- pray with persons who have special needs
- lead a prayer group at your workplace

Ministries within the church:

- be a prayer partner to believers in a specific ministry
- be part of a prayer group
- help develop a prayer ministry

Community-oriented ministries for Christ:

- pray for local and national governments
- become a prayer partner to a parachurch agency
- start a neighborhood prayer ministry

Potential Liabilities in the Gift of Intercession

A person with this gift can sometimes tend to

- become mechanical in the use of prayer lists.
- take pride in much praying and look down on others who don't pray for hours at a time.
- assume that prayer is a substitute for action.

Intercession as a Responsibility of All Christians

Every Christian is called to pray for others. "Pray for each other," writes James; "the prayer of a righteous person is powerful and effective" (James 5:16). "Devote yourselves to prayer, being watchful and thankful," Paul charged the Colossians (Col. 4:2). Prayer is required of all believers so that all may "stand against the devil's schemes" (Eph. 6:11). After urging believers to put on the whole armor of God, Paul concludes, "Pray in the Spirit on all occasions with all kinds of prayers and requests. With this in mind, be alert and always keep on praying for all the Lord's people" (Eph. 6:18).

Exploring Intercession from Scripture

1. What are some of the results of intercessory prayer, according to

   - Ephesians 6:18-20?
   - 1 Timothy 2:1-4?
   - James 5:16b-18?

2. What place did intercessory prayer have in the church, according to James 5:14-16?

3. What is the Holy Spirit's role in the prayers of believers? (See Romans 8:26-27.)

4. What was the tenor of Paul's prayers for members of the churches he had planted (Eph. 1:15-19; Phil. 1:3-11; Col. 1:9-12)? What difference do you suppose it made in the lives of those believers to know that they were prayed for?

KNOWLEDGE

Definition

The Spirit-given ability to receive from God knowledge that is crucial to ministry and that could not have been obtained in other ways.

Knowledge as a Spiritual Gift

In Greek the word for "a message of knowledge" in 1 Corinthians 12:8 means literally "a deep knowing." The New Testament does not make clear whether this means learned knowledge or revealed knowledge. Scholars interpret the meaning both ways. Peter Wagner defines this gift as "the ability . . . to discover, accumulate, analyze, and clarify information and ideas" (*Your Spiritual Gifts Can Help Your Church Grow*). Bob Whitaker, however, says this gift "is not about intellectual ability or learning; it is an inner knowing or intuition such as was seen in Jesus' ministry when he knew what his critics were thinking, feeling, or plotting, and then spoke in response as though he had read their minds" *(In the Spirit's Power;* see Mark 2:8; Luke 6:8; 7:36-47; 9:47).

While no one can say exactly what Paul had in mind in 1 Corinthians 12:8, there are reasons to believe that he was talking about knowledge or information received directly from the Lord. First, such a meaning fits well into this context in which the other gifts mentioned have a strong supernatural dimension. Second, often in the Old Testament and at least fifteen times in Jesus' ministry and seven times in Acts we observe this kind of knowledge being received directly from God. In other words, we observe the gift in use. In each case the knowledge was crucial to ministry.

The knowledge that this gift brings is probably not the same as that connected with the special revelation of the Bible (see 2 Tim. 3:16). Nor is this knowledge intended to add to what Scripture teaches. It is essentially guidance: knowledge or information given by the Holy Spirit that relates to a specific situation or moment. Its application relates mainly to a specific context in which the Spirit intends to guide or minister for the glory of God. This localized "message of knowledge" is subject to the truth of Scripture and does not contradict it. It should also be tested by a larger community or leadership group.

For examples from the Bible, see Peter's confession of Christ in Matthew 16:15-17 and Paul's comments in Ephesians 3:1-6.

The communication revealed in the gift of knowledge may come in various forms, such as feelings, words, nudges, images, insights, thoughts, impressions, or a word of Scripture that will penetrate one's thoughts (see Heb. 4:12-13). The gift is supernatural to the extent that the information received could not have been obtained in a way other than from God, who knows all things.

Characteristics of the Person with the Gift of Knowledge
- has received from God a knowledge of things that would happen before they actually came to pass
- has experienced God-given, supernatural insights while praying

Some Ways to Use the Gift of Knowledge
Personal/informal uses:

- use God-given information to help a person whom the Lord has brought into your life
- counsel others who are making long-term decisions

Ministries within the church:

- preach or teach with effectiveness because the Lord has given you a special awareness of a need or of particular issues
- be part of a healing ministry team with Christians who have other gifts for such a ministry

Community-oriented ministry for Christ:

- serve as a volunteer with a counseling agency
- work with an evangelistic team

Potential Liabilities in the Gift of Knowledge

A person with this gift can sometimes tend to

- become puffed up because of insights discerned and messages revealed.
- communicate publicly a word of knowledge that was meant to be private.
- fake the word of knowledge when no revelation has come.

Knowledge as a Responsibility of All Christians

It is necessary for every believer to have knowledge of God's revelation. For those who are not given knowledge as a spiritual gift, the knowledge of God's revelation will come primarily through study of the Word of God and through those who preach and teach. Often when a person is reading or hearing God's Word, the Spirit will impress a particular truth upon the individual or give heightened insight and understanding of the Scriptures. Careful and diligent study of the Word of God will help every believer grow spiritually and be effective in ministry.

Exploring Knowledge from Scripture

1. Read Matthew 16:13-17. What word of knowledge did Peter receive?

2. How did knowledge help Jesus to minister effectively to a Samaritan woman? (See John 4:17-19; see also John 2:24-25.)

3. What is the message of knowledge referred to in Ephesians 3:1-6? How significant was this for Paul's ministry?

LEADERSHIP

Definition

The Spirit-given ability to lead others by seeing and casting a ministry vision, setting and communicating goals, and inspiring and directing people to work together toward those goals.

Leadership as a Spiritual Gift

The Greek word in Romans 12:8 that denotes leadership as a gift of the Spirit identifies a person who "stands before," rules, leads, or directs. The help given by the leader is often for the well-being of the persons led. The leader cares for, provides for, and sees to the needs of people involved together in a ministry function. The leader is also very much a servant. The tense of the verb in Romans 12:8 suggests that the leader participates in the activity being led. The leader is a kind of "player-coach," as some Bible scholars put it.

Romans 12:8 states that the one who leads must do so "diligently." Diligence involves doing one's best, exerting oneself, putting forth an intense effort. Paul's diligence in leading is evident in 2 Thessalonians 3:7-9: "We were not idle when we were with you, nor did we eat anyone's food without paying for it. On the contrary, we worked night and day, laboring and toiling so that we would not be a burden to any of you."

Nehemiah is a good example of a spiritually gifted leader who exercised his gift. He cast a vision for rebuilding the walls of Jerusalem, established and communicated goals to accomplish the task, and inspired and directed those who followed him to work together toward a common purpose (see Neh. 2:11-20; 4:14; 12:27-43). Nehemiah was also a gifted administrator (see Neh. 4:11-13, 16-23). (See the gift study on administration for a comparison of leadership and administration as different yet related gifts.)

The Bible teaches that those who are chosen to lead or rule must demonstrate their ability first in their own homes (1 Tim. 3:4). Elders are to "direct the affairs of the church" (1 Tim. 5:17) and serve as "shepherds of God's flock . . . watching over them—not because [they] must, but because [they] are willing, as God wants [them] to be; not pursuing dishonest gain, but eager to serve; not lording it over those entrusted to [them], but being examples to the flock" (1 Pet. 5:2-3). The Scriptures also speak to those who are led: "Acknowledge those who work hard among you, who care for you in the Lord and who admonish you. Hold them in the highest regard in love because of their work" (1 Thess. 5:12-13).

Characteristics of the Spiritually Gifted Leader
- able to provide the overall vision for a task
- used by God to motivate others who willingly follow and work together in a kingdom project
- serve effectively by setting clear goals and involving people in working toward those goals

Some Ways to Use the Gift of Leadership
Personal/informal uses:

- manage your own family life well
- lead your family in a project
- help a friend set long-term objectives

Ministries within the church:

- chair a committee
- cast the vision for a new ministry and see that it meets its goals
- help the church establish long-range plans

Community-oriented ministries for Christ:

- give leadership in a service agency
- serve on a steering committee for a new retirement home
- serve in political office

Potential Liabilities in the Gift of Leadership

The spiritually gifted leader can sometimes tend to

- be insensitive to those involved in carrying out details of the vision.
- get too far ahead of the people being led.
- take pride in position or power.
- make projects more important than people.
- be more authority-conscious than ministry-conscious.

Leadership as a Responsibility of All Christians

The leader is a person who is usually a step or two ahead, sets goals, and motivates people toward those goals. Every Christian has these responsibilities in one way or another. Parents lead their children. Mature Christians lead new Christians. Elders and deacons lead in the church. All Christians should look ahead and set goals for their own spiritual development. The importance of planning for the future was surely in Jesus' mind when he spoke of counting the cost before building a tower (Luke 14:28-30). Paul was concerned to make goal-oriented planning a part of every Christian's life when he spoke of pressing on "toward the goal to win the prize for which God has called [us] heavenward in Christ Jesus" (Phil. 3:14). In this sense, all Christians have leadership responsibility.

Exploring Leadership from Scripture

1. What was the role of church leaders as noted in Hebrews 13:7? How were followers to benefit from their leaders?

2. What qualifications for leadership did David have (Ps. 78:72)?

3. Describe in your own words the attitude required of a leader as shown by Jesus in Luke 22:24-27.

4. What characteristics of a good leader are apparent from 2 Thessalonians 3:7-10?

Gift Studies

MERCY

Definition
The Spirit-given ability to feel empathy and compassion for hurting people and to translate that feeling into cheerful acts of service.

Mercy as a Spiritual Gift
People with the spiritual gift of mercy cheerfully and effectively show Christ's love and compassion as they reach out to people who suffer. Daniel Fuller defines mercy as "compassion so great that it stoops to aid even the most pitiable and undeserving." The gift involves a deep and extraordinary compassion that transcends normal human caring.

Believers who have the gift of mercy help people who are sick, aged, physically or cognitively impaired, homebound, poor, homeless, imprisoned—any who are in troubled situations. Mercy is also extended to those who are spiritually unhealthy and in bondage to Satan. In fact, our acts of mercy may be our best witness to people outside the kingdom of God (Matt. 25:34-40).

The person with this gift not only feels deeply but is moved to action. Jesus demonstrated mercy by reaching out to the sick, suffering, and outcast people of his day. In one of Jesus' most famous parables, a good Samaritan shows compassion toward a helpless victim and pays the price of involvement at great risk and cost to himself (Luke 10:30-37). Dorcas, a devoted follower of Christ, combined feeling and action in her use of the gift of mercy. She was "always doing good and helping the poor" (Acts 9:36). James points out that mercy should not simply be caring but also sharing: "Suppose a brother or sister is without clothes and daily food. If one of you says to them, 'Go in peace; keep warm and well fed,' but does nothing about their physical needs, what good is it?" (James 2:15-16).

Characteristics of the Person with the Gift of Mercy
- feels deeply for hurting people and is eager to give practical help
- enjoys helping people who suffer physical, mental, or emotional troubles
- effective in ministering to hurting people

Some Ways to Use the Gift of Mercy
Personal/informal uses:

- help a sick neighbor
- send cards to persons with special needs
- be a good listener

Ministries within the church:

- visit persons who are homebound or in a nursing home
- help stock an emergency food pantry
- be an advocate for people who have disabilities or impairments

Community-oriented ministries for Christ:

- volunteer to work at a psychiatric hospital
- be a nursing-home helper
- become a foster parent to physically challenged adults
- be involved in a crisis-pregnancy center

Potential Liabilities in the Gift of Mercy

People with this gift can sometimes tend to

- see only good motives in others, who may take advantage of the giver's help.
- respond emotionally without looking at all the facts.
- be overly protective of the people cared for.
- lose a sense of their own boundaries in working with Christians who have other gifts.

Mercy as a Responsibility of All Christians

Many Bible passages emphasize mercy as a responsibility of all Christians. The Old Testament prophet Micah announced this as God's intent: "He has shown all you people what is good. And what does the LORD require of you? To act justly and to love mercy and to walk humbly with your God" (Mic. 6:8). Jesus said, "Blessed are the merciful, for they will be shown mercy" (Matt. 5:7), and, "Be merciful, just as your Father is merciful" (Luke 6:36). In his parable of the good Samaritan, Jesus shows that mercy involves a readiness to help a hurting person (Luke 10:30-37). This readiness is required of all believers.

Exploring Mercy from Scripture

1. Read Romans 12:8 and write out the phrase that identifies the gift of mercy. With what attitude must the gift be exercised?

2. Look through Luke 4-8 for examples in which Jesus showed mercy. What examples do you find?

3. What insights can we gain from Luke 6:36 and James 2:15-16 about showing mercy?

4. Read Matthew 25:34-40. To whom is the merciful person really ministering when doing deeds of mercy? What difference does that make?

MIRACLES

Definition

The Spirit-given ability to serve as an instrument through whom God performs extraordinary works as an expression of his presence and power.

Miracles as a Spiritual Gift

The gift of miracles is identified as a spiritual gift in 1 Corinthians 12:10, which speaks of "miraculous powers." Verse 28 of the same chapter adds that "God has placed" miracles "in the church"—that is, in "the body of Christ" of which we are all a part (12:27).

Much of the teaching about healing can also be applied to miracles. Many of the astonishing healings done by Jesus were miracles. However, the gift of healing primarily addresses illnesses or maladies, and the gift of miracles deals more often with laws of nature.

Writing in *I Believe in the Holy Spirit*, Michael Green suggests that the miracles Paul had in mind in 1 Corinthians 12 were focused mainly on casting out demons. John Calvin agrees, adding that God "in his severity uses miracles for the destruction of Satan" (Calvin's *New Testament Commentaries: The First Epistle of Paul to the Corinthians*). Paul's imposition of blindness upon the magician Elymas (Acts 13:9-11) and the deaths of Ananias and Sapphira (Acts 5:1-11) are evidence of God's miraculous severity.

Jesus regularly used the gift of miracles in his ministry. His miracle-working powers were gift powers from God, not simply an exercise of his divinity. Jesus explained that his power to cast out demons was by the Spirit of God (Matt. 12:28). Among his miracles were turning water into wine (John 2:1-11), calming the wind and sea (Mark 4:35-41), walking on water (Matt. 14:22-32), feeding more than five thousand people (Matt. 14:13-21), and raising people from the dead (Mark 5:35-43; Luke 7:11-15; John 11:38-44). The disciples also worked miracles, using this spiritual gift in Jesus' name (Acts 3:1-10).

The purposes for miracles are many. Jesus worked miracles to attest to his claims as the Messiah (Acts 2:22) and to show the great love and power of God (John 6:30-40) revealed in the coming of his kingdom (Mark 1:15). In addition, "signs, wonders, and miracles" were among "the marks of a true apostle" (2 Cor. 12:12). Christ promised to enable believers to do great things in response to their asking so that "the Father may be glorified in the Son" (John 14:12-14). The author of Hebrews reminds us that it was "by signs, wonders and various miracles, and by gifts of the Holy Spirit" that God testified to the gospel (Heb. 2:3-4).

Many Western Christians have difficulty believing that miracles are part of God's plan today and that they still occur. Our Western worldview tends to exclude this possibility. Christians today should cultivate an awareness of God's miraculous ways by meditating on his miracles of the past, being open to evidence of miracles in today's world, praying that God will work miracles to increase his kingdom on earth, and stepping out in faith and obedience to serve God in whatever work he calls us to.

Characteristics of the Person with the Gift of Miracles

- confidence that God can and does work miracles today, having seen it happen
- used by God to show his miraculous power in a situation where ordinary means were not sufficient
- serve as God's instrument in opposing the devil through God's mighty power

Some Ways to Use the Gift of Miracles

Personal/informal uses:

- in a desperate situation where there is no possible human solution, ask God for a miracle

Ministries within the church:

- teach others about the spiritual gift of miracles
- stand ready to assist church leaders who face impossible situations

Community-oriented ministries for Christ:

- lead the church to contest spiritual strongholds that grip the community
- through God's power, challenge evil where it is entrenched in society

Potential Liabilities in the Gift of Miracles

A person with this gift can sometimes tend to

- try to work a miracle without being guided by the Spirit of the Lord.
- take personal credit for work that only the Lord could do.
- look down on others who do not have this gift.

Working Miracles as a Responsibility of All Christians

Since the power displayed in a miracle is not the power of humans but that of the sovereign Lord, God may choose to use any Christian to work a miracle. All believers should remain open to this possibility and trust that almighty God can use any humble, believing, obedient Christian in this way. Lack of openness and lack of faith can thwart God's desire to use us or bless us through miracles (Matt. 13:58).

Exploring Miracles from Scripture

1. Miracles are among the mighty works of God in the Old Testament, such as the plagues in Egypt (Ex. 7-12), the Red Sea crossing (Ex. 14:21-22), the collapse of Jericho's walls (Josh. 6:1-20), the survival of three friends in a fiery furnace (Dan. 3), and many more. According to Psalm 145:3-7, what is the purpose of such mighty works?

2. How did miracles serve to advance the kingdom of God, according to the following passages?

   - John 3:2; 9:16; 20:30-31
   - Acts 5:1-11
   - Acts 12:1-17
   - Acts 13:6-12
   - Hebrews 2:4

3. Read John 14:12-14. Who is able to do the mighty works of God? How? When? Why?

PROPHECY

Definition

The Spirit-given ability to receive and communicate a message from God so that believers may be edified and encouraged and unbelievers convinced.

Prophecy as a Spiritual Gift

The Greek word for *prophesy* means "to speak forth." The word *prophet* in both Hebrew and Greek is defined as "one who speaks for another." Prophecy is the message spoken by the prophet. God, the source of the message, conveys his thoughts to the prophet. Through the prophet God speaks to his people. Before the Scriptures were completed, prophets often received direct revelation. Today the Bible is the prime source of prophetic message—but, of course, the Spirit is free to give guidance as through the prophets of biblical times (see Acts 11:28). When the Holy Spirit does speak directly to an immediate situation today, it will not contradict the revealed Word of God in Scripture.

The gift of prophecy is mentioned in every one of the major gift passages in Scripture. Paul considers prophecy a most valuable gift that should be eagerly desired by believers (1 Cor. 14:1). When prophets speak, hearers must be careful not to "put out the Spirit's fire" and not to "treat prophecies with contempt" (1 Thess. 5:19-20). By means of this gift, believers are built up and encouraged, and by it the church is edified (1 Cor. 14:3-5).

Prophecy was a foundational gift for the New Testament church, which is "built on the foundation of the apostles and prophets, with Christ Jesus himself as the chief cornerstone" (Eph. 2:19-20), and it is one of the gifts God uses to equip believers for ministry (Eph. 4:11-13). The prediction of future events, though often a possibility by means of the prophetic gift, is not the main focus of the prophet's work. The main purpose of prophecy is to speak the word of God so that people understand God's will for them in the place and time they are living in. The main focus of prophecy today is on Christ, the Word of God himself (John 1:1, 14), whose good news of salvation is for all who believe (Rom. 1:16-17). The rightful place of prophecy is Christ's body, the church, made up of God's people everywhere.

The words of prophecy must always be tested, for prophets can err. In a book titled *In the Spirit's Power*, Bob Whitacker says,

> [Prophecy] is a reporting in human words what God has put on our minds. It is a mix of God and human; it is more or less pure and powerful depending upon God's initiative and the receptivity, motives, and spiritual maturity of the speaker. Prophecy, like sermons, can be poor, good, or excellent. That is why it needs to be weighed.

In 1 Corinthians 14:29-33, Paul explains how to weigh what prophets speak. John advises us to "test the spirits to see whether they are from God, because many false prophets have gone out into the world" (1 John 4:1; see also vv. 2-3). Jesus himself similarly warns against false prophets (Matt. 7:15-16).

Characteristics of the Spiritually Gifted Prophet
- used by God to plead the cause of God to the people of God
- used by God to build up and encourage other Christians by speaking to them of spiritual things
- used by God to proclaim timely and urgent messages or to give directions that have come through God's Word and/or Spirit

Some Ways to Use the Gift of Prophecy

Personal/informal uses:

- underscore the truth of God's Word to a friend
- lead family and friends to an awareness of God's will for their lives today
- give guidance received from the Holy Spirit to other believers

Ministries within the church:

- preach a scripturally based message with compelling application to contemporary needs
- instruct a class studying current social problems
- give direction that affects a congregation's future

Community-oriented ministries for Christ:

- speak out publicly on important moral or social issues
- write about political and social issues from a biblical perspective

Potential Liabilities in the Gift of Prophecy

Persons with this gift can sometimes tend to

- take personal pride in their ability to speak persuasively.
- deviate from or go beyond the Scriptures (1 Cor. 14:37-38).
- be so negative as to be prophets of doom rather than bearers of the good news of Jesus.
- be so blunt that people are put off by their manner.

Prophecy as a Responsibility of All Christians

In a sense, all Christians are prophets. Prophecy involves a "speaking forth" of God's truth in the world we live in. All Christians are responsible to speak out and show the truth of God in their lives even if they are not extraordinarily gifted to do so. Moses expressed a desire in line with this, saying, "I wish that all the LORD's people were prophets and that the LORD would put his Spirit on them!" (Num. 11:29). The prophet Joel predicted that God would pour out his Spirit "on all people" and that the "sons and daughters" of God's people would prophesy (Joel 2:28-29)—and this word from the Lord was fulfilled on Pentecost (Acts 2:16-17). Paul counseled believers to aim for a broad use of prophecy, saying, "I would rather have [every one of] you prophesy" (1 Cor. 14:5); he even envisioned a worship service in which "everyone [was] prophesying" (14:24).

Gift Studies

Exploring Prophecy from Scripture

1. How was prophecy used in Acts 15:31-32?

2. What happened through prophecy as reported in Acts 13:1-3?

3. How should prophets conduct themselves in public worship, according to 1 Corinthians 14:29-33?

4. What warnings and encouragements do we find in Matthew 7:15-16 and 1 John 4:1-3?

SERVICE (HELPING)

Definition

The special Spirit-given ability to see and meet the needs of others by willingly helping them in practical ways.

Service as a Spiritual Gift

Wherever we look in the home, the church, or the community, we see hundreds of things that need tending to. Many of these things require no more than the ability to identify a task and the willingness to get it done. That's essentially what the gift of service is about—seeing and meeting needs. The needs or tasks may be menial or unattractive to others, but they are willingly assumed by the person with the gift of service. The Greek word for "service," *diakonia*, as in Romans 12:7, has its roots in a word meaning "to run errands."

As a spiritual gift, *diakonia* (service) is shown most clearly in those who make themselves available to reach out to a personal or material need. Jesus modeled this gift best by coming "not . . . to be served, but to serve" (Mark 10:45). Phoebe, "a deacon [servant] of the church," exhibited the gift of service by being "the benefactor [kind, great helper] of many people" (Rom. 16:1-2). Titus demonstrated the gift of service by enthusiastically carrying money gifts collected for the needy in Jerusalem (2 Cor. 8:16-19).

In Scripture the gift of service is also described as the gift of helping others (1 Cor. 12:28). The idea in helping others is basically the same as service. Helping involves taking a burden on yourself instead of leaving it on someone else.

The gift of service must not be regarded as unimportant because it doesn't seem to require special skills in a way like some other gifts do. It's a valuable gift sorely needed in the church. Jesus himself emphasized this gift when he said, "I am among you as one who serves" (Luke 22:27), and,

"I have set you an example that you should do as I have done for you" (John 13:15).

Characteristics of the Person with the Gift of Service

- enjoys doing tasks that help others minister effectively
- is not put off by menial tasks but does them willingly to help build up the body of Christ
- finds practical ways of helping others, and enjoys doing so

Some Ways to Use the Gift of Service

Personal/informal uses:

- be a helper in all kinds of ways for family members and neighbors
- help a busy single parent with childcare
- assist someone who needs an extra hand with a difficult task or project

Ministries within the church:

- help out in the nursery
- do kitchen work for church functions
- be involved in a refugee-resettlement program
- help meet the needs of members who are sick, disadvantaged, or poor

Community-oriented ministries for Christ:

- take part in a community clean-up effort
- remodel homes for disadvantaged families
- work in a used-clothing center

Potential Liabilities in the Gift of Service

Persons with the spiritual gift of service can sometimes tend to

- become "worried and upset about many things" and ignore the importance of other things needed to build up the body of Christ (see Luke 10:41-42).
- never say no, get overinvolved, and then feel they are being used.
- use their gift to gain the appreciation of others.
- neglect home and family while serving others.

Service as a Responsibility of All Christians

All Christians are responsible to serve. They are challenged to be "the servant of all" (Mark 9:35) and to live like their Lord, who came "not . . . to be served, but to serve" (Matt. 20:28). All believers have a duty to "help the weak" (1 Thess. 5:14), says Paul, and to "serve one another humbly in love. For the entire law is fulfilled in keeping this one command: 'Love your neighbor as yourself'" (Gal. 5:13-14).

Exploring Service from Scripture

1. What liability in the gift of service do we learn from the story of Mary and Martha in Luke 10:38-42?

2. How did Phoebe's life and ministry illustrate the gift of service? (See Rom. 16:1-2.)

3. What do we learn from Jesus about the gift of service? (See Matt. 20:28; Mark 9:35; Luke 22:27; John 13:15.)

4. With what attitude did Stephanas and his household serve the church, according to 1 Corinthians 16:15-18? What difference did their ministry make in the church?

SHEPHERDING (PASTORING)

Definition

The Spirit-given ability to watch over, care for, and feed members of the body of Christ, guiding, admonishing, and discipling them toward spiritual maturity.

Shepherding as a Spiritual Gift

Shepherding is identified as a gift because the Greek word for "pastor" or "shepherd" is found in Ephesians 4:11 among the list of gifted persons who serve the church. Often this gift is called pastoring. We use the word "shepherd" here to avoid confusing the gift with the position of the professional pastor. A person does not need to be an ordained pastor or to be theologically trained in order to exercise this gift.

A person who has the gift of shepherding may hold the formal position of elder or overseer (see 1 Tim. 3:1-2; Greek: *episkopos;* also translated as "bishop"). The terms for "shepherd," "elder," and "overseer" ("bishop") seem to be interchangeable in Scripture. Most likely they give us three different views of a single ministry role. The word "shepherd" speaks of the person who ministers pastorally, caring for, guiding, and watching over the "flock" of God's people (1 Pet. 5:2-3). The word "elder" points to one's honored place, being held in esteem for wise counsel, in the community. And the word "overseer" describes aspects of both of these terms.

The person who has the gift of shepherding watches over, cares for, feeds, guides, and protects other believers (Isa. 40:11; John 21:16-17; Acts 20:28-29; 1 Pet. 5:2). The shepherd will ordinarily be "able to teach"

(1 Tim. 3:2; Eph. 4:11) and will be able to "encourage others by sound doctrine and refute those who oppose it" (Titus 1:9). A shepherd is also called to equip and enable others so that they may be built up and grow into Christlike maturity (Eph. 4:12-13). Persons gifted as shepherds do their work willingly and eagerly, operating not with heavy-handed authority but by means of a good example (1 Pet. 5:1-3).

Characteristics of the Spiritually Gifted Shepherd

- assumes responsibility for the spiritual well-being of others, guided by the Holy Spirit
- enabled by the Spirit to provide ongoing care, spiritual nourishment, and protection to other believers
- used by God to watch over and guide other Christians and nurture them toward spiritual maturity

Some Ways to Use the Gift of Shepherding

Personal/informal uses:

- disciple a new convert
- guide a friend or neighbor toward spiritual growth
- disciple family members

Ministries within the church:

- become a youth group counselor
- serve as an elder
- lead a discipling class
- lead a small group

Community-oriented ministries for Christ:

- conduct a prison ministry
- do volunteer work for a child-guidance clinic
- lead campus Bible studies or faith-nurture groups

Potential Liabilities in the Gift of Shepherding

Persons with the gift of shepherding can sometimes tend to

- have difficulty saying no to additional involvement in ministering pastorally.
- be so sensitive that they will not confront people who need admonition.
- allow the people to whom they minister to become overly dependent.

Shepherding as a Responsibility of All Christians

A shepherd is one who tends a flock by feeding, guiding, leading, and watching over sheep. There is a sense in which every Christian is called to be a shepherd. All are to care for one another (1 Cor. 12:25), guide one another (Prov. 11:14; 15:22), and seek the welfare of one another (Phil. 2:1-4), as a shepherd does for his sheep. The lambs of the flock require special concern (Matt. 10:42; Mark 9:42). Parents are shepherds to their children. Teachers of children shepherd them with loving care. Youth counselors, coaches, and high school vocational counselors shepherd their charges through many situations. Not all of the persons in these positions have the gift of shepherding. Many are simply exercising a responsibility out of a heart of love.

Exploring Shepherding from Scripture

1. What is the task of the shepherd/pastor as described in Ephesians 4:11-13?

2. What are the significant things we learn about a shepherd's role from Jesus in John 10:1-18?

3. What do we learn about the shepherd's task from Ezekiel 34:1-6, 11-16? What will happen if the shepherd fails?

4. In 1 Peter 5:1-4 the shepherd is an elder of the church. What must the shepherd do? How? What is the shepherd's reward?

TEACHING

Definition

The Spirit-given ability to clearly and effectively communicate biblical truths and information to help believers grow in faith, building up the body of Christ.

Teaching as a Spiritual Gift

In 1 Corinthians 12:28 we find the gift of teaching associated with gifts such as prophecy and miracles. In Ephesians 4:11-12 it is closely associated with shepherding (pastoring), given to the church "to equip [God's] people for works of service, so that the body of Christ may be built up." In Romans 12:7 we find it associated with prophesying, encouraging, serving, and giving. Teaching is a very useful, practical gift for building up the people of God and helping everyone learn about God and "grow in the grace and knowledge of our Lord and Savior" (2 Pet. 3:18).

Jesus clearly exercised this gift. We read that "when Jesus saw the crowds, he went up on a mountainside . . . and began to teach them" (Matt. 5:1-2). Jesus' teaching was clear and effective. He used the stuff of everyday life—sheep, wine, water, candles, seeds, yeast, and so on—to illustrate difficult teachings about the kingdom. His parables attracted and held the attention of his audiences. After Jesus ascended to heaven, the Holy Spirit took up a teaching ministry, as the Lord had promised: "The Advocate [Counselor], the Holy Spirit, whom the Father will send in my name, will teach you all things" (John 14:26).

The apostles whom Jesus had chosen to carry on his work and to lay the foundation of the church also exercised the gift of teaching. "They never stopped teaching and proclaiming the good news that Jesus is the Messiah" (Acts 5:42). The apostle Paul, even while under house arrest in Rome for the sake of Christ and the gospel, "welcomed all who came to see him . . . proclaimed the kingdom of God and taught about the Lord Jesus Christ" (Acts 28:30-31).

The Bible gives a few cautions about teachers and teaching. Believers are warned, "Not many of you should presume to be teachers . . . because you know that we who teach will be judged more strictly" (James 3:1). Peter cautions, "There will be false teachers among you. They will secretly introduce destructive heresies, even denying the sovereign Lord. . . . Many will follow their depraved conduct and will bring the way of truth into disrepute" (2 Pet. 2:1-2).

Most of what was written in the gospels and letters of the New Testament came from believers who exercised the gift of teaching. Again and again, this gift was used to make Scripture's (and thus the Holy Spirit's) urgent appeals to practical Christian living. Teaching remains a much-needed gift in the Christian community today.

Characteristics of the Spiritually Gifted Teacher
- able to explain the Bible or some aspect of Christian living in an instructional setting, guided by the Holy Spirit
- able to communicate truth clearly and effectively in such a way that others learn
- able to hold the interest of people being taught

Some Ways to Use the Gift of Teaching
Personal/informal uses:

- teach your own children Bible truths
- lead a friend in a one-to-one Bible study
- clarify religious issues for a neighbor

Ministries within the church:

- serve as a church school teacher
- lead an adult Bible study
- lead lessons as part of a small group

Community-oriented ministries for Christ:

- teach school
- instruct in a life-enrichment class

Potential Liabilities in the Gift of Teaching

A spiritually gifted teacher can sometimes tend to

- be more concerned with head knowledge than heart knowledge.
- communicate too much information too quickly.
- be more content-oriented than student-oriented.
- assume that those being instructed have a high interest in the subject.

Teaching as a Responsibility of All Christians

To teach is to impart knowledge to others. All Christians, whether by actions or words, do this. "By this time you ought to be teachers," says the writer of Hebrews, admonishing immature Christians (Heb. 5:12). And to all Christians Paul says, "Let the message of Christ dwell among you richly as you teach and admonish one another with all wisdom" (Col. 3:16). The whole church is given a teaching role in Jesus' challenge to make disciples, "teaching them to obey everything" that Jesus himself has taught (Matt. 28:20). The Bible, in fact, is our fundamental source for "teaching . . . and training in righteousness" (2 Tim. 3:16). "Everything that was written in the past was written to teach us," says Paul, "so that through the endurance taught in the Scriptures and the encouragement they provide we might have hope" (Rom. 15:4).

Exploring Teaching from Scripture

1. Read Acts 18:24-28. What can we see in Apollos's example that tells us about the gift of teaching?

2. What can keep the gifted teacher from pride? (See 1 Cor. 3:5-9; James 3:1.)

3. Read Acts 20:18-21; 28:30-31. What can we see in Paul's example that tells us about the gift of teaching?

4. What is the goal of teaching, according to Ephesians 4:11-14?

Gift Studies

TONGUES (Speaking and Interpretation)

Definition
The Spirit-given ability to speak in a language previously unknown to the speaker and/or to interpret for the benefit of the church.

Tongues as a Spiritual Gift
The gift of tongues is clearly reported in Scripture. It was given to the company of believers on Pentecost day (Acts 1:15; 2:1-4), to the family of Cornelius after they responded to Peter's preaching (Acts 10:46), and to a group of Ephesian believers (Acts 19:6). The apostle Paul also spoke in tongues and expressed his desire that other Christians might be able to do so (1 Cor. 14:5, 18). In some cases the tongue that is spoken is a language understood by someone else present, as at Pentecost. In other cases the tongue-speaking may be direct communication with God (1 Cor. 14:2; see also 13:1).

In the biblical reports, tongues were used in two different ways. In 1 Corinthians 14:2 we read that tongues is a form of prayer or praise language to God. The believer uses tongues in personal devotions as a form of intimate, direct communication with God that transcends human interpersonal communication. It has the effect of deepening and enriching one's prayer life and building up one's faith. This use of tongues may also take the form of spiritual song (1 Cor. 14:14-15; Eph. 5:19). Paul desires that everyone would speak in tongues (1 Cor. 14:5), suggesting that it is a desirable gift for every believer.

While the gift of tongues is valuable, it is also potentially problematic. Paul warns that tongue-speaking can be disruptive and divisive. Without love the gift is useless (1 Cor. 13:1). In public worship the use of tongues should be limited, and interpretation should be available (14:27). If there is no one to interpret, the tongues should not be spoken for others to hear (14:28). Believers who speak in tongues should pray for the gift of interpretation (14:13). In public worship, prophecy is recommended over tongues for its value in bringing understanding (14:18-19, 24). Balance is important. Believers who pray in tongues should pray with the mind also (14:15-17). Those who have experienced tongues and interpretation of tongues say that the interpretation is usually not a word-for-word translation but instead gives the sense of the message.

Once interpreted, tongues are basically equivalent to prophecy. The guidelines that apply to prophecy also apply to the interpretation of tongues. (See the gift study on prophecy earlier in this section.)

Gift Studies

The Bible teaches that tongues is also a "sign gift." In 1 Corinthians 14:22 Paul specifically notes that this gift is a "sign . . . for unbelievers" when tongues are used in worship. The tongues spoken at Pentecost demonstrated the effects of this sign. Startled and amazed by what they heard the apostles speaking, the crowd asked, "What does this mean?" (Acts 2:12). Then Peter spoke God's Word to the crowd (prophecy), and as a result many people were converted and brought into the church that day (Acts 2:14-41). In such a context, speaking in tongues serves as a sign of the presence and power of God and grabs the attention of those present so that they can hear God's Word and come to repentance (see 1 Cor. 14:23-25).

Here are some cautions to keep in mind. First, the gift of tongues is not usually associated with extreme emotion or ecstasy. The speaker remains in control and can choose when and where to exercise the gift (1 Cor. 14:27-30). Further, although tongues often accompanies a personal experience of empowerment by the Holy Spirit, it is not to be considered the initial evidence of being filled with the Holy Spirit, as some people claim. Neither is it a special mark of spiritual maturity. Finally, to avoid overemphasizing the gift and its value, remember that speaking in tongues was never a major emphasis of Jesus or his disciples. The Bible includes no reference to Jesus speaking in or interpreting tongues.

Characteristics of the Person with the Gift of Tongues

- prays in an unknown language or in a way that goes beyond expression with words
- is built up in faith by use of this gift
- understands what God is saying when someone speaks in tongues
- used by God to edify worshipers by interpreting tongues
- has spoken in tongues and has received an interpretation of them

Some Ways to Use the Gift of Tongues

Personal/informal use:

- in personal devotions
- quietly in public worship
- receive an interpretation from the Holy Spirit when privately speaking in tongues

Ministries within the church:

- in public worship when an interpreter is present, and others can "weigh carefully what is said" (1 Cor. 14:29)
- interpret tongues spoken in public worship so that everyone may be edified

Community-oriented ministries for Christ:

- praying for neighbors in a neighborhood prayer ministry
- reporting to the community any interpretation that is meant for them

Potential Liabilities in the Gift of Speaking in Tongues

The person with this gift can sometimes tend to

- use the gift for self-glory or superiority over others.
- make speaking in tongues the norm for spiritual maturity.
- pretend to have an interpretation and keep it from others.

The Gift of Tongues as a Responsibility of All Christians

Many Christians who are both mature and effective in ministry have never spoken in tongues. That's not a problem. In 1 Corinthians 12:30 Paul's questions "Do all speak in tongues? Do all interpret?" assume a negative answer. Underlying the practical expressions of this gift, however, are spiritual values that all believers are responsible for, such as praising God in prayer, yielding control to the Holy Spirit, and speaking for Christ in ways that gain the attention of unbelievers.

The key issue in tongues is that of receiving a message directly from God that will edify the body of Christ. Though most Christians will not likely possess this gift, all should be as open as possible to impressions the Holy Spirit may desire to give in order to build us up. Jesus said, "My sheep listen to my voice" (John 10:27). Jesus regularly heard and responded to the voice of the Father.

Exploring the Gift of Speaking in Tongues from Scripture

1. Acts 2:1-4; 10:44-47; and 19:1-6 describe Spirit outpourings on groups of early believers that resulted in speaking in tongues. What do these events have in common? In what ways do they differ?

2. Read 1 Corinthians 14:2, 4, 22, 26. Why has God given tongues to the church?

3. What cautions and controls does Paul recommend in the following passages?

   - 1 Corinthians 13:1
   - 1 Corinthians 14:13-17
   - 1 Corinthians 14:27-28

4. How does the gift of tongues compare to prophecy, according to 1 Corinthians 14:1-6, 18-19, 22?

Gift Studies

WISDOM

Definition
The Spirit-given ability to see situations and issues from God's perspective and to apply God-given insights to specific areas of need.

Wisdom as a Spiritual Gift
The spiritual gift of wisdom mentioned in 1 Corinthians 12:8 is the ability to apply knowledge in a fitting way to the glory of God. The person with this gift often helps to solve a difficult problem, offers pertinent spiritual counsel, knows how to handle a difficult person, or helps bring reconciliation between alienated persons.

Jesus possessed and exercised this gift. People were impressed by the wisdom with which he spoke (Mark 6:2). His perspective was clearly given him by the Father in heaven (Matt. 11:25-27). His words of wisdom shone through in the perceptive answers he gave to people who tried to trap him (Matt. 21:23-27; 22:23-33; Luke 20:20-26). We see the Lord's wisdom most clearly in the cross (1 Cor. 1:18-25). No wonder Paul said that in him "are hidden all the treasures of wisdom and knowledge" (Col. 2:3).

The disciples were promised special wisdom in moments of special challenge (Luke 12:12; 21:14-15), and they gave evidence of possessing this gift in the situations Jesus described (Acts 3:11-4:20). The apostle Paul also wrote his letters with God-given wisdom (2 Pet. 3:15).

The source of all wisdom is God himself, as Scripture reminds us in Proverbs 2:6, "The Lord gives wisdom," and in 1 Corinthians 2:13, "We speak, not in words taught us by human wisdom but in words taught by the Spirit, explaining spiritual realities with Spirit-taught words." Divine wisdom is contrasted with worldly wisdom, which is "foolishness in God's sight" (1 Cor. 3:19).

Characteristics of the Person with the Gift of Wisdom
- gives practical insights to people that help to solve problems
- receives insight from God in situations for which there was no previous knowledge
- able to apply spiritual knowledge in practical ways

Some Ways to Use the Gift of Wisdom
Personal/informal uses:

- counsel friends who come for help with their problems
- apply scriptural principles to one's own life

Gift Studies

- live out the truth of James 3:17: "The wisdom that comes from heaven is first of all pure; then peace-loving, considerate, submissive, full of mercy and good fruit, impartial and sincere."

Ministries within the church:

- serve as a member of a counseling team
- help guide the body of Christ through a troublesome time
- be available to members of the church who may be facing financial difficulties, family problems, business reversals, and so on

Community-oriented ministries for Christ:

- serve in a governmental or judicial position or as a counselor to such officials
- serve as an arbitrator or negotiator between sparring parties or groups
- serve on a jury

Potential Liabilities in the Gift of Wisdom

A person with this gift can sometimes tend to

- become overly self-confident and begin to offer human wisdom rather than godly wisdom.
- think of oneself too highly.
- become impatient with people who don't listen to the wisdom of God.

Wisdom as a Responsibility of All Christians

All believers are called to "get wisdom" (Prov. 4:7), and the person who finds it is blessed (Prov. 3:13-14). God offers wisdom to all who please him (Eccles. 2:26). James declares that wisdom is available to all who need it and ask for it in faith (James 1:5-6). Jesus promises wisdom to all who are tested (Luke 21:15). The wisest thing a Christian can do is to hear the words of Christ and live by them (Matt. 7:24).

Exploring Wisdom from Scripture

1. What can we learn from Matthew 21:23-27 about Jesus' use of this gift? From Luke 20:20-26?

2. What do we find in Acts 4:8-13, 18-20 to indicate that Peter and John had the gift of wisdom? (See also Luke 21:15.)

3. What is one purpose of the message of wisdom, according to Colossians 1:28?

4. Read James 3:13-17. What distinguishes a truly wise person from a worldly wise person?

FOLLOW-UP TOOLS

WAITING GIFTS SURVEY

About the Waiting Gifts Survey

Some of our gifts may be "gifts in waiting," or "waiting gifts." These are gifts that we have not used (much) in ministry but that are waiting to be developed. If you have little ministry experience and have struggled to discover spiritual gifts that you are using, this survey may help you identify gifts that God is working to develop in you. Then, when you have discovered your waiting gifts, look for opportunities to confirm them by using them with others in ministry.

Even though you may not use or be aware of your waiting gifts now, there will be hints of them in your daily living. Waiting gifts can often be identified by answering questions that help measure your interests, inclinations, sensitivities, attitudes, and concerns.

How to Complete the Survey

This survey uses a scale of 0-7 (with 7 as the strongest value) to help you state how strongly each statement describes you. Read each statement and circle the number that shows **how strongly you identify with the statement** (how often this is true of you, how deeply this is true of you, and so on). Work quickly. Don't worry about giving a "wrong" answer; your first impressions are usually correct.

It will take about 15-20 minutes to complete this survey.

Tally Results for Later Use

When you have completed the survey, figure out your results by using the key chart on page 124 and following the instructions there. You'll need to refer to these results in session 5, and your group leader may want to collect them for reference and ministry follow-up later.

Learn More

Once you've discovered your waiting gifts, learn more about them in the Gift Studies section of this book. Take time also to learn about other gifts so that you can recognize and appreciate the gifts of others. Remember that the purpose of discovering your gifts is to serve well together as the body of Christ, to the glory of God and his kingdom.

On a scale of 0-7 (with 7 as the strongest value), indicate how strongly each statement describes you.

1. I have a sense for delegating important tasks to the right people at the right time.

   0   1   2   (3)   4   5   6   7

2. I am drawn to people with creative abilities, and I see them as examples of what I want to be and do.

   0   1   (2)   3   4   5   6   7

3. I can usually tell whether a person is lying.

   0   1   2   (3)   4   5   6   7

4. I would like to be able to help people overcome things that keep them from achieving their potential.

   0   1   (2)   3   4   5   6   7

5. I am concerned for people who are far from God, and I want them to know Christ.

   0   1   2   (3)   4   5   6   7

6. I sense that God may intervene in a situation even when that seems unlikely.

   0   1   2   3   (4)   5   6   7

7. I am moved when confronted by a need, and I want to help as much as I can.

   0   1   2   3   (4)   5   6   7

8. I am sensitive to others' hurts and want to be involved in their healing in some way.

   0   1   2   (3)   4   5   6   7

9. I enjoy meeting people and have a knack for making them feel comfortable in social situations.

   0   1   (2)   3   4   5   6   7

10. When I see people in need or hear about them, I am drawn to pray for them.

    0   1   2   3   (4)   5   6   7

11. I sometimes receive information that's helpful in real-life situations and seems to come from God.

    0   1   2   (3)   4   5   6   7

12. I tend to notice when a project group is "spinning its wheels" and needs clear direction.

    0   1   (2)   3   4   5   6   7

13 I am drawn to people who are hurting, and I want to help them.

    0   1   2   (3)   4   5   6   7

14 I get excited that God "is able to do immeasurably more than all we ask or imagine," and I want to participate in God's powerful actions.

    0   1   2   (3)   4   5   6   7

15 I have a desire to communicate insights I have received from God's Word by the Holy Spirit.

    0   1   (2)   3   4   5   6   7

16 I am quick to notice things that need to be done, and I don't mind offering help.

    0   1   2   (3)   4   5   6   7

17 I tend to tune in and want to help when people need counsel or guidance.

    0   (1)   2   3   4   5   6   7

18 I like to help people learn new things or get a better understanding of things they already know.

    0   1   (2)   3   4   5   6   7

19 Sometimes when I pray, I reach a point where familiar words cannot express my thoughts and feelings.

    0   1   (2)   3   4   5   6   7

20 I often know what to do and how to do it in situations where others are puzzled.

    0   (1)   2   3   4   5   6   7

21 In a group I am often the one who tries to develop a plan of action.

    0   (1)   2   3   4   5   6   7

22 I would like to develop the musical, artistic, literate, or drama abilities that I sense in myself.

   (0)   1   2   3   4   5   6   7

23 I tend to notice when people are pretending to be what they are not.

    0   1   (2)   3   4   5   6   7

24 I tend to see potential in people, and I look for ways to help them grow.

    0   1   (2)   3   4   5   6   7

25 I am moved when people come to faith in Christ, and I thank God for their salvation.

    0   1   2   (3)   4   5   6   7

26 I tend to accept God's promises at face value and apply them to given situations without doubt.

    0   1   2   3   (4)   5   6   7

27 I want to cut back on expenses when I know my donations really make a difference in helping people.

    0   1   (2)   3   4   5   6   7

28 I would be pleased to be used by God in helping to heal others.

    0   1   2   (3)   4   5   6   7

29 I am sensitive to how people feel in unfamiliar situations, and I try to find ways to help them feel at ease.

    0   1   2   (3)   4   5   6   7

30 I have an inner conviction that God works in response to prayer, and I want to be used to help others through prayer.

    0   1   2   (3)   4   5   6   7

31 I seem to know things because God has somehow revealed them to me.

    0   (1)   2   3   4   5   6   7

32 I am surprised how often people pick up on my ideas when I suggest a course of action.

    0   (1)   2   3   4   5   6   7

33 I have always been one to notice and reach out to people who are hurting.

    0   1   2   (3)   4   5   6   7

34 When I know of a need or concern, I imagine God working a miracle to solve the problem.

    0   1   2   (3)   4   5   6   7

35 I sense the need to speak God's message of hope and vision in situations of injustice, wrong, or confusion.

    0   1   (2)   3   4   5   6   7

36 I wish I had more opportunity to assist others in their ministries.

    0   1   (2)   3   4   5   6   7

37 I find myself wanting to give direction to people who seem to be off course.

    0   (1)   2   3   4   5   6   7

38 I am concerned when people are confused, and I want to help clarify things for them.

    0   (1)   2   3   4   5   6   7

39 The Spirit has nudged me at times to explain a message given in tongues.

   (0)   1   2   3   4   5   6   7

40 When I am faced with a difficult situation, I find myself asking, "What is God's perspective in this?"

    0   1   (2)   3   4   5   6   7

KEY CHART

How to Use the Key Chart

Fill out the key chart on the next page after completing the waiting gifts survey.

1. In the space next to each number in the key chart, enter the score (0-7) that you assigned to each of the 40 statements in the survey.

2. Add up the scores in each row, and enter the total in the far-right column.

3. Cross out the gifts you identified earlier as your working gifts from the Spiritual Gifts Survey that you completed earlier in this course. Here you want to identify gifts that have high scores but are not already known to be your working gifts.

4. Circle the three highest remaining scores listed in the Total column. These are your three strongest waiting gifts.

5. Write the names of these gifts in the blanks at the bottom of the page, listing them from highest scored to lowest. In case of a tie, give a higher rating to the gift that you sense is more dominant. Remember that although the remaining gifts may not be your strongest, you still have a responsibility in each gift area.

6. Hand in or send your results to your group leader or gifts administrator. You may want to use the Ready to Serve! form (p. 126) for this purpose.

Key Chart

Spiritual Gift	Responses		Total
Administration	1 _3_	21 _1_	_4_
Creative Ability	2 _2_	22 _0_	_2_
Discernment	3 _3_	23 _2_	_5_
Encouragement	4 _2_	24 _2_	_4_
Evangelism	5 _3_	25 _3_	_6_
Faith	6 _4_	26 _4_	_8_
Giving	7 _4_	27 _2_	_6_
Healing	8 _3_	28 _3_	_6_
Hospitality	9 _2_	29 _3_	_5_
Intercession	10 _4_	30 _3_	_7_
Knowledge	11 _3_	31 _1_	_4_
Leadership	12 _2_	32 _1_	_3_
Mercy	13 _3_	33 _3_	_6_
Miracles	14 _3_	34 _3_	_6_
Prophecy	15 _2_	35 _2_	_4_
Service (Helping)	16 _3_	36 _2_	_5_
Shepherding (Pastoring)	17 _1_	37 _1_	_2_
Teaching	18 _2_	38 _1_	_3_
Tongues (Speaking and Interpretation)	19 _2_	39 _0_	_2_
Wisdom	20 _1_	40 _2_	_3_

My Waiting Gifts

Highest scored gift _faith_

2nd _Intercession_

3rd _Mercy + Healing_

READY TO SERVE!

Name: _____

Date: _____

Enter your results in the spaces on this form. These responses help to
identify the types of service God has in mind for you. This form will serve
as a record of your gifts, interests, and passions as a result of taking this
course. This form will also help your ministry leaders suggest ways for you
to serve God in line with your gifts, talents, and passions.

1. Spiritual Gifts
Working gifts:

_____   _____

_____   _____

Waiting gifts:

_____   _____

_____

2. Interests/Skills/Talents for Ministry
Remember the exercise from lesson 3 about confirming your spiritual gifts?
Jot down two or three answers you came up with under point 3, "Analyze
Yourself" (p. 37).

3. Ministry Passions

On the basis of your responses about ministry passions in session 5 (see p. 47), how would you describe your top two or three passions for doing ministry in connection with your spiritual gifts?

4. Availability

I believe I can contribute about _____ hours to ministry in my church and community each week.

You have permission to photocopy this form for church office or administrative use in helping you find opportunities to serve in ministry.

BIBLIOGRAPHY

Calvin, John. *New Testament Commentaries: The First Epistle of Paul to the Corinthians.* Translated by John W. Fraser. Edited by David W. Torrance and Thomas F. Torrance. Grand Rapids, Mich.: Eerdmans, 1960, 1989.

Clifton, Donald O. and Marcus Buckingham. *Now, Discover Your Strengths.* New York: Free Press, 2001.

_____ , Albert L. Winseman, and Curt Liesveld. *Living Your Strengths.* Second edition. New York: Gallup Press, 2004.

Green, Michael. *I Believe in the Holy Spirit.* Grand Rapids, Mich.: Eerdmans, 2004.

Harrison, Everett F., Geoffrey W. Bromiley, and Carl F.H. Henry, eds. *Baker's Dictionary of Theology.* Grand Rapids, Mich.: Baker Book House, 1960.

O'Connor, Elizabeth. *Eighth Day of Creation: Discover Your Gifts.* Revised edition. Washington, D.C.: Potter's House, 2007.

Snyder, Howard A. *The Community of the King.* Downers Grove, Ill.: InterVarsity Press, 2004.

_____ . *The Problem of Wineskins: Church Structure in a Technological Age.* Downers Grove, Ill.: InterVarsity Press, 1975.

_____ . *Radical Renewal: The Problem of Wineskins Today.* Revised edition. Eugene, Ore.: Wipf and Stock Publishers, 2005.

Wagner, C. Peter. *Your Spiritual Gifts Can Help Your Church Grow.* Ventura, Calif.: Regal Books, 2005.